AF430174

DELVINGS

DELVINGS

Italy, Sex, Heresy, Astronomy,
and Other Things…

Edward Alberic Gosselin

WELTANSCHAUUNG GESCHICHTE
Jacksonville, Oregon
2024

Published in 2024 by
Weltanschauung Geschichte
Jacksonville, Oregon

Designed and produced
by Lucky Valley Press
www.luckyvalleypress.com

DEDICATION

To Jois

and

To my children, Elisabeth Ryen
and David Gosselin, and to my
grandchildren, Hudson and Harper
Ryen, and Cayden, Ryder, Dylan, and
Londyn Gosselin.

Contents

"Truth is the correspondence of facts to reality."

– Ludwig Wittgenstein
Tractatus Logico-Philosophicus

Introduction

My Cat Blackie and a Historian's Delvings

When I was a kid growing up in Rutland, Vermont, I had a cat named Blackie. He was different from other cats. He would not catch mice and eat them, so my dad had to catch them in mouse traps and give them to him. He also wouldn't eat cat food; he would only eat dog food.

He was kind of a hapless cat, until we moved away from Rutland to Meriden, Connecticut, when I was nine years old. We couldn't take Blackie with us. My mother told me that they had given Blackie to the veterinarian, and that Blackie was participating in research experiments with the vet.

After that we would periodically return to Rutland to visit my grandparents. I would ask my mother if we could go to the vet and see Blackie. She always said he was much too busy with his research experiments at the vet's clinic to have time for visitors. This is how things stood for several years. I was very proud of Blackie. He had come into his own and was an important cat.

Perhaps that's why I first wanted to be a medical doctor. I could participate in medical research and help people just as Blackie was helping other cats. People would ask me why I wanted to be a doctor. "To help people," I always replied.

But then my mother finally told me: Blackie had been "put to sleep." He had not been helping other cats with research. As far as I know, that was the only mistruth my mother ever told me.

That's when I dropped the idea of becoming an MD and I began instead to want to delve into the truth of things. And that's how I eventually became a historian.

This book is an example of seeking truth, of historical delving. It brings together five different subjects which I have thought, taught, and written about in my career as a historian. I have never stopped pondering and refining my ideas on these topics. And so the following chapters are fresh insights into my delvings.

One might at first think that these chapters do not have a connecting tissue. But they form integral contextualizations when they are brought together: they all examine how topics or subjects change over time and, in so doing, form part of the multiverse of human thought. Thought is the central point here, for all these chapters in *Delvings* relate to intellectual history or, as it is sometimes also called, the history of ideas or, in its German cognate, *Weltanschauung Geschichte*.

During my thirty-four year tenure at California State University, Long Beach, and subsequent semesters teaching in the History Department and then in the OLLI Program at Southern Oregon University, my favorite courses were the intellectual history of the Renaissance and of the Reformation; History and Theory; Modernization theory; and the History of Science. *Delvings* focuses on aspects of four of those courses[1]. The chapter on the making of Italy and Italians is most closely related to themes that were found in my course on Modernization theory; that on Foucault stems from themes I began to develop in a required upper-division course on History and Theory; the chapter on the sixteenth-century runaway heretic monk, Giordano Bruno, stems from my interest not only in Renaissance humanism and philosophy, but also from preparing a seminar on a comparison of the thought of Bruno and Galileo; lastly, the chapters on the history of science and on Proxima Centauri b fully develop themes some of which I only touched on in my interdisciplinary course on these subjects.

Having indicated these connections of the chapter subjects with my teaching career, I must add that the following chapters do not precisely reprise anything I have already said in lectures or writing. In fact, these chapters are new interpretations of my previous work on each of these subjects. They come from continued research and thought—delvings— over the past several years since my retirement.

The findings of my individual delvings are found in the following chapters:

---

1. I have previously published *The Reformation (History in an Hour),* published by HarperCollins, 2012.

Italy

It is well known that the Italian peninsula was not united under a single ruler until 1861 (1870, when papal Rome was finally added to the new Italian state). One could argue that this unification of the multitudinous Italian cities and city-states into one political entity was an important step in the modernization of Italy. However, that unification did not make all the peoples of Italy feel Italian. That achievement has been a long process and, I would suggest, it may not even yet be concluded. An Italian meeting a foreigner is still more apt to say that she is Venetian, Florentine, Calabrian, etc., than that she is Italian. And the new Italian government contains parties that may well want to break asunder the unified Italian state itself.

Foucault

To understand the relevance of the famous and important twenti-eth-century French philosopher-historian, Michel Foucault, we must ascertain his place in relation to the development of French historians in the twentieth century (the *Annales* School) and to the late nine-teenth-century German philosopher, Friedrich Nietzsche. In addition, Foucault's final publications as a historian were tightly related to his own personality and sexual orientation. We will find that this personal orientation caused Foucault to recast completely what he had projected in 1976 would be in his History of Sexuality and to end it with emphasis on confession and final forgiveness for the innate concupiscence of all humans since the Fall of Man.

Bruno

As suggested above, I have long been reading, studying, and writing about the Italian apostate monk, Giordano Bruno—thought errone-ously by many to have been among the first modern scientists, predat-ing Galileo by a few years; and also to have been a hero of Italy because of the way he, amidst the flames of his execution at the stake, violently turned his head away from the Holy Crucifix that was held up for him to see and to beg forgiveness in his final moments before his consump-tion by the flames. Over the years, I have recast my view of Bruno as a troublesome and heroic philosopher to that of him being a rebellious monk who aspired to recreate the Roman Catholic religion into one in which he would be its new and real Messiah. His ultimate goal was literally a spatially infinitudinous religion, stretching far beyond the bonds of Earth.

Science

Chapter Four is a long survey of the development of exact mathematical astronomy from the Late Babylonians (c. 350 BCE) to the Michelson-Morley Experiment (1887) and Einstein's *Special Theory of Relativity* (1905). Along the way, we consider the science and thought of Euclid, Ptolemy of Alexandria, Galileo, Kepler, Paracelsus, and Newton, to name only a few. One of the questions raised in this chapter is whether there was a singular Scientific Revolution of the Seventeenth Century, or whether the development of exact mathematical astronomy has been ongoing since the late Babylonians. The history of science became my most treasured course topic in the last years of my teaching. This chapter has a special dedication: to my son David whose love of math inspired me to become interested in exact mathematical astronomy.

A History of the Future

The last chapter explains why human beings may have to leave the Earth and settle on a far-off exoplanet such as on Proxima b in the con-stellation Centaurus. Proxima b is the closest exoplanet to Earth that may be habitable by humans. But it will take about 6,300 years to get there, in other words many generations will live and die in the "space buses" that transport millions of earthlings and their descendants to Proxima b. Life will be difficult there. This is a History of the Future.

Although these chapters deal with different topics, they form a panoply of ideas which are all tightly related not just to human thought but to the way in which thinking humans structure their sev-eral worlds and form, withal, a cultural history as they proceed from birth to death. Alas, not all members of human society think deeply, or sometimes even at all. But we must hope that humans and their societal cultures can, as a whole at least, advance rather than decline and fall—whether on Earth or on some other far-off planetary abode.

. . .

I am indebted to the National Endowment for the Humanities which facilitated my academic year as a Fellow in the National Institute for the Humanities at the University of Chicago (1977-8) under Edward W. Rosenheim and Harry Harootunian; through this position I was introduced to the issue of Modernization. My interest and expertise in Michel Foucault, one of the twentieth-century's most influential French philosophers, began in Spring, 1976, when I was an *auditeur* in Foucault's course, "Il Faut Défendre la Société," at the Collège de France in Paris. My work and interest in Bruno began with my studies with Eugene F. Rice, Jr. and Paul Oskar Kristeller at Columbia University as well as with my friendships with Frances Yates of the Warburg Institute at the University of London, and Allen G. Debus at the University of Chicago. Lawrence S. Lerner and I joined in the 1970s to translate, edit, and publish Giordano Bruno's *La cena de le Ceneri* (1584) and to develop courses, with the support of NEH Demonstration Grants in 1973 and 1974, for our Program on the History of Science in the Physics and History Departments at CSULB. I should note that History of Science was not at that time commonly taught outside of elite research universities such as Chicago and Yale, and Dr. Lerner and I were excited to bring this field of learning to our own students at Long Beach. The Mellon Foundation Summer Seminars at Stanford University (1980, 1981) led to my study of Nietzsche and Foucault. An NEH summer seminar in 1985 under the directorship of Asger Aaboe and a subsequent summer grant at Yale in 1986 honed my understanding of ancient and medieval exact mathematical astronomy. Influenced as I have been by these people and organizations, I would like to emphasize that any errors in this book are mine alone.

My deepest gratitude is to my beloved wife, Jois Harkness, who has encouraged me in all ways, intellectual and otherwise.

– E.A.G.

CHAPTER ONE

MAKING ITALY AND
MAKING ITALIANS

A Misunderstood Sign
on the Road from Malpensa Airport

I took my thirteen-year-old daughter, Elisabeth, on a trip to Italy in 1992. We landed at Malpensa Airport and were met by cousin Carlo Barberis, who drove us into Milan where he and his wife lived. Along the highway, I saw a white sign with big black lettering that read *"Lega Nord,"* i.e., "Northern League." I thought back to the history of the Middle Ages and supposed that the sign might refer to the area of the league of Lombard or northern Italian City States that defeated the Holy Roman Emperor Frederick I (Barbarossa or Red Beard) at the Battle of Legnano in 1176.

I asked Carlo if the sign was an historical marker about that medieval Lombard League. He chuckled and said, "No, it means this is the area of the political party known as the Northern League for the Secession and Independence of Padania." It was a right-wing, populist party that wanted northern Italy to become an independent state, separate from Italy.

Clearly, I thought, Italy as we know it could cease to be Italy, and the people in the northern half of the Italian peninsula could become Padanians. This would include the citizens of Piedmont, Liguria, Lombardy, the Veneto, and the Alpine region of Italy. The party had been founded in 1991, and Matteo Salvini, the future Deputy Prime Minster of Italy, was one of its leaders.

And so by this sign on the road from Malpensa Airport to Milan, we are introduced to the ongoing problem of "making Italy and Italians." It is a problem, however, that is not dissimilar to the problem of the making of France and Frenchmen between 1880 and 1914 or, even now, it would seem, the continuing problem of making the United States and Americans. So let us delve into the problem of making Italy and Italians. It is, in a sense, a model for other national histories and even political theories.

Making Italy
and Making Italians

The Ongoing Attempt
at State Formation

In 1994 I gave a presentation to an upper-division Italian class on the modern history of the Italian state and people. This chapter is a further examination of that topic.

PART I

The visitor to Italy might be surprised at how often she might hear people speaking varieties of Italian. There is, for example, a Venetian dialect, a Roman dialect, a Calabrian dialect, and multiple micro dialects as you go from town to town. For example, an Italian friend from the Veneto once told me that each town around Venice has its own dialect, and not just Venice itself.

More than dialects, at one time there were entirely different major languages spoken in the Italian peninsula. I begin by mentioning these facts — and will come back to them in more detail shortly — in order to underline a more important fact, that ITALY is really a quite recent and still unfinished fabrication.

The Italian peninsula was first united as a confederation of cities under the leadership of the Roman Republic and Empire. But starting in the fifth century CE and throughout the next eight hundred years, the peninsula was divided into three main areas: the Kingdom of Italy in the north, under the Holy Roman Emperor; the Papal States in the center, under the control of the Bishop of Rome (the Pope); and the Kingdom of Naples, under the control of a king who at one time was of Neapolitan blood, and at another time, of Spanish Hapsburg blood. The Kingdom of Naples included the island of Sicily, which was also dominated at one time by the French as well as by the Arabs.

After the battle of Legnano in 1176, the northern League of Italian city states defeated the forces of the Holy Roman Emperor, Frederick Barbarossa (the Red Beard), and thereby gained their independence from the Empire. The cities that became independent city-states were Milan, Genoa, Venice, Florence, Lucca, Pisa, Bologna, and other smaller communes. Each one was an independent sovereign state. Their inhabitants never said they were Italian; they said they were Milanese, Genoese, Florentine, and so forth. During the Renaissance (1340-1600), some of the smaller, independent states were swallowed up militarily or

economically by more powerful states — such as Florence, Milan, and Venice. This political situation persisted until the seventeenth century, when Spanish Hapsburg princes ruled much of northern and southern Italy. There flousished in the nineteenth century a movement called the Risorgimento, at first inspired by Napoleon's victories in northern Italy (1796-7) whereby General Bonaparte created meritocratic and democratic governments in the liberated cities. The goal of the Risorgimento was to unite all of the Italian peninsula under one ruler or prince.

Il Risorgimento

In 1843, the Italian peninsula was divided into a series of sovereign city-states. By 1871 the peninsula had become a single state under Vittorio Emanuele II. How did this come about? In part, the unification of Italy that started in 1861 was part of a larger nineteenth-century movement of modernizing state formation. Wilhelm I, the King of Prussia, and his powerful prime minister, Otto von Bismarck, created the united German Reich in 1871. Similarly, the formation of a singular Italian state was accomplished by the King of Savoy and Sardinia, Vittorio Emanuele II and his prime minister, Camillo di Cavour.

Vittorio Emanuele II

Camillo Benso Cavour di Ciseri

The Italian unification movement had begun earlier than the nineteenth century. Petrarca (Petrarch) in his 1344 poem, "My Italy," had spoken of the way the "green land" of the Italian peninsula was blocked off from the "German madness" by the "shield of the Alps." And Machiavelli's *The Prince* two centuries later called for a prince, a leader, who would unify the peninsula. These were dreams in the form of what might be called a cultural nationalism.

Alessandro Manzoni

In the nineteenth century, the call for unification took on real and exuberant form. Giuseppe Mazzini (1805–1872) tried to agitate the call for revolution in Italy. He was expelled from his home town, Genoa, and finally spent many years in London, still calling for revolution and the unification of Italy under an Italian leader. Alessandro Manzoni (1795–1872) published his great novel, *I promessi sposi (The Betrothed)* in 1826. It was written in the Lombard dialect. When he republished it twenty years later, he had gone to Florence, and learned Tuscan. His republication was in Tuscan, which he thereby helped to make the Italian national language. The greatest monument to Manzoni was Verdi's magnificent *Requiem* which was composed to honor his memory.

Notwithstanding that the leaders of the *Risorgimento* dreamed of a unified republic, this kind of state (despite General Bonaparte's republican constitutional city-state reforms in 1796-7) was not in the offing for the mid-nineteenth-century Italian peninsula. The King of Savoy's prime minister, was a shrewd political operator. He used another great nationalist dreamer, Giuseppe Garibaldi (1807–1882) and his red-shirted army to fight to unite Italy and drive out, in

Giuseppe Garibaldi

Petrarch's earlier words, "the barbarians," i.e., the Spanish Hapsburg and Bourbon rulers of northern and southern Italy. Rome, Venice, Trieste, and Trent were not yet under the King of Savoy's control in 1861 when he became King of Italy. But when Garibaldi's troops finally liberated Rome of papal control in 1870, all of the Italian peninsula was finally united under the King of Italy. The capital, first situated in Torino (Turin) in 1861, was moved to Rome in 1870.

When Garibaldi conquered Rome in 1870, Pope Plus IX lost his dwindling papal political power, and was basically captivated in the small 110 acres of Rome known as Vatican City. And so the modern Italian state was formed — all of Italy, with the Pope's political power minimized in the 44 hectares of the Vatican. Some historians have argued that the doctrine of papal infallibility was defined dogmatically at the First Vatican Council of 1869–1870 in order to replace the Pope's lost political status with this new theological doctrine.[1]

The Problems of
"Making Italy"and "Making Italians"

The new King of Italy and his Prime Minister said, "We have made Italy. Now we must make Italians." This was a formidable task and was, as we will see, more easily said than done.

In 1870, Italy was still composed of very different regional societies, all with different economies, linguistic cultures, and histories. Even to say that the new Kingdom of Italy was composed of a variety of regional societies is to speak too broadly. There were many economic and cultural differences within Sicily alone — Arab, French, German, land barons, wretched poverty, and the newly formed farmland. The rivalry between the towns of Tuscany in the north was proverbial. The provincial regions of southern Italy were "invented" in 1864 by the statistical office in Torino: Abruzzo, Molise, Campania, Apulia, Basilicata, and

---

1. See John Herman Randall, Jr., *The Making of the Modern Mind: A Survey of the Intellectual Background of the Present Age* (New York: Columbia University Press, 1940), 545: "In 1869 Pius IX called the first ecumenical council since Trent [sixteenth century], which in 1870 *at the very moment the Italian troops were thundering at the gates of Rome* [my italics], proclaimed the new dogma of Papal Infallibility. This dogma represents the irrevocable commitment of the Church against liberal tendencies. It was not a new doctrine, having been taught by Thomas Aquinas and the Jesuits, but it had never before been made binding doctrine (*de fide*)."

Calabria. There was no cohesion in southern Italy. Parts of it were barely Christian and still very much pagan. Furthermore, nation building and the "making of Italians" were hampered by the economic backwardness of the region, from the Abruzzo south to Calabria. Nation building was further hampered by the hostility of the Catholic Church and its clergy to the anti-Church Italian state (at least until Mussolini's Concordat with the Church in 1929), and by the fact that most Italians could not read or write.

Indeed, this was probably the central problem of "making Italians." People could barely speak the national Italian language of Tuscany that had developed since the Renaissance period, or understand what anybody from another region was saying. There were several minority linguistic groups scattered throughout the country: 80,000 French speakers in the Valle d'Aoste; 96,000 Albanian and 30,000 Greek speakers in the South; 30,000 Slav speakers in Friuli and Molise. These 236,000

Vittorio Emanuele II

completely different foreign-language speakers formed only one percent of the population, and they weren't the real problem. Most of the other 99% spoke regional dialects and nothing else. This was true even among the upper classes. For example, Vittorio Emanuele II, the king of the newly unified Italian state, spoke Piedmontese. His famous remark when entering Rome in 1870, which history textbooks record as "*Ci siamo e ci resteremo*," was actually spoken in a dialect much closer to French: "*Finalment i suma*."[2]

In most of Italy, what we today know as Italian was a dead language, used sometimes for literary purposes by the intellectual elite, especially in Tuscany. Outside of Rome and Tuscany-Florence, perhaps only 0.6% of the peninsular population knew Italian in 1870. If you include Tuscany-Florence and Rome, then about 2.5% out of the total

---

2. "Finally we are here."

Italian population of 26.8 million knew Italian. The other 97.5% of the Italian population had no common language. And there were few social or political links among the various micro-regions of the peninsula. Many aspects of late nineteenth-century Italian history—the difficulty of eradicating illiteracy, the minuscule circulation of newspapers and journals—become understandable if you remember that Italians did not normally speak the same language and couldn't communicate with one another. This helps explain Italian immigration to the United States and elsewhere in the nineteenth and early twentieth centuries: why remain in Italy if you could immigrate and learn to be with foreign peoples who were linguistically no more strange to you than people two villages away in Italy itself?

Even today there are small pockets of people in Calabria in the South who are descendants of Greeks who settled in southern Italy and eastern Sicily in the sixth century BCE, and again under the Eastern Roman Emperor Justinian in the sixth century CE, and still again when Greeks fled the Byzantine Empire after its fall in 1453 to the Ottoman Turks. These currently remaining Greeks in Calabria call themselves *Greki* and their language *Greko.* They do not call themselves Italians. Their language is not modern Greek as it is heard in Athens, but a variant dialect, developed over centuries past in their isolated areas. It is not Italian either. This shows still another of the problems of "making Italians."[3]

How then to "make Italians?" What incentives were there to become literate in Italian, the obscure national language, or to insure that young children become literate? There was no popular press, and since very little was written in the various dialects and languages of the multitudinous micro-regions, it seemed useless for most Italians to try to learn reading or to speak a national language, or even to learn to read and write in their local patois. Those who emigrated from Calabria, Sicily, Naples, and so forth became known as Italians only in their new lands, while they never had seen themselves as such in the parts of Italy they had come from; and then it seemed sensible for them to learn a new national language, be it French, German, or English, because that was the only way they could hold jobs and follow orders in factories in their new lands.

---

3. See *Istoria*/Life (August 14, 2017).

(The situation wasn't very different in other European states. In France, for example, what we know today as French was only spoken in a small area surrounding Paris — the Île de France. Once outside that area around Paris, other dialects, even other languages, were spoken: Celtic in Brittany; Provençal in southern France near Italy; and Languedocian in south-western France from Toulouse to the Pyrenees. Parisian French was known as "langue d'oui" (the language where they said "oui" for yes); Languedocian or langue d'oc" was the language where they said "oc" for yes.)

Interestingly enough, in both Italy and France, the institution that ultimately most successfully taught the national language was the army. Only conscripts in the armies of Italy and France had a real motive to learn to read, write, and speak Tuscan Italian and Parisian French, for otherwise they would not be able to follow orders, nor could they hope to have a career in military service after serving their time as conscripts.[4]

Education, Brothels, and Other Forms of Leisure

In the 1870s and 1880s, there was a tradition of lay education only in Piedmont and Lombardy. Throughout the rest of the Italian peninsula there was scarcely a tradition of any kind of education, whether lay or church. In 1877, there were only two years of compulsory education. In 1888, the compulsory education requirement was extended to three years. However, the legal requirement to attend school for two or three years was still largely a fiction. In southern Italy, truancy was well above eighty per cent. Peasant children were needed at home to work in the fields or to tend flocks, and they could only sporadically be spared for anything as ephemeral as schooling.

Few periodicals catered to leisure interests because most southern Italians simply did not have the time for them. The rural leisure that did exist in the south focused on the traditional feast days of the Catholic Church and on their sacred dramas and processions. Religious processions with a statue of the Virgin Mary at its front always excited the people: "There's the Virgin;" "Here comes the Virgin," people would shout, as they drew as close as they could to the passing statue. They thought of the statue as being the Virgin herself, and not a facsimile. About the

---

4. Cf. Eugen Weber, *Peasants into Frenchmen: The Modernization of Rural France, 1870-1914* (Stanford: Stanford University Press, 1976.)

only non-religious recreation available were wine shops, though wine was expensive. There were always the brothels, and they were commonly frequented by men of all classes, and were used by fathers to introduce their sons to sexual behavior. Entertainment was also to be had from balladeers and musicians on the streets, much as you might still find in Naples today. Small-scale circuses, bearded ladies, sword swallowers, quack-medicine sellers, and hermaphrodites made the rounds from village to village, again especially in the south, and they could be found in the criminal sub-world. Fellini's 1954 movie, *La Strada*, gives a quite accurate picture of rural, southern Italian and Sicilian life.

In sum, popular leisure in late nineteenth-century Italy was traditional and unsophisticated. This point is clearer if we look at what was not available. At the time when working-class Englishmen were flocking to the seaside for a vacation, Rimini on the eastern coast of Italy was still a small provincial town, and Ostia, on the western coast near Rome, was a malarial swamp.

The picture was different for the urban middle and upper classes in northern cities. They patronized the theater, in part because it was one of the only places well-bred ladies could be seen in public. Of course, this was the golden age of Italian opera. Verdi's *Aida* premiered in 1871; *Otello* premiered at La Scala Milan in 1887; and his *Falstaff* was first performed in 1893. These were obviously unlike lower-class leisure activities of balladeers and bearded ladies in southern Italy and Sicily. Northern Italians of the middle and upper classes attended opera much as their class compatriots in Vienna, Berlin, and Paris did in the nineteenth century.

The most characteristic middle-class leisure institution — as also in France — was the café. It afforded the only informal meeting occasions for middle-class men, just as the wine shops did for peasants and artisans. It was in the cafés where the few newspapers that were published were read, that politics was discussed, and that public opinion was formed. The cafés were places where middle-class values were created and diffused, and where the new ruling groups of united Italy developed both the senses of self-confidence and of being right that are required for the comfortable exercise of power over others. In other words, the cafés were places where "Italians were made," at least for middle-class Italians in the cities of Piedmont, Lombardy, and Tuscany.

"High Politics" and "Low Politics," "Il Problema del Mezzogiorno," and the Great War

When we turn to politics from 1870 to the present, we are faced with the problem of the Italian state having to decide just how its political institutions would function. This is another aspect of the problem of "making Italy." The modern Italian state has experienced two types of political modalities: historians have termed them "high politics" and "low politics."[5] "High politics" largely dominated the Italian state from 1870 to the fall of Fascism in 1943 and the end of the monarchy (by referendum) in 1946. Since then, Italy has been a republic and has until recently followed the path of "low politics." This is not a distinction between moral and immoral politics. Rather, it is a distinction between two choices about where governmental power and decision-making should rest.

"High politics" from 1870 to 1946 meant that power in the state emanated from the king, and it was shared by his appointed prime ministers and the army. The parliamentary politicians always had to accept the king's foreign policy, however much they disliked it. The alternative was to undermine the monarchy and thus the unity of Italy. This was a classic recurring pattern. The kings, up to World War One, left most of foreign policy to their diplomats. They could not be too bothered by foreign policy, for they did not have enough money for a good war.

In as much as the kings up to 1913 were interested in the army, it was because the army could be used internally in the kingdom to instill the discipline and patriotism needed, in their view, to hold a fractured Italy together. The army was used against internal enemies of the state: brigands, rioters, strikers, anarchists, and all those holding illegal assemblies. A "state of siege" was declared ten times between 1861 and 1922 to quell all forms of domestic disharmony. State-building was thus the task of the army. But the army's prestige was undercut because of its acts of repression, and it was popularly hated by the people.

The rulers of the state, from the king through the upper ranks of the civil service were Piedmontese. This very fact undercut national unity, for the people from the other areas of Italy saw the ruling

---

5. Denis Mack Smith, *Italy: A Modern History* (Ann Arbor: University of Michigan Press, 1959).

class as something they could not enter and therefore as their enemy. Parallel institutions came to rival the state institutions: the marginalized brigands, strikers, and protesters. These were all committed to anti-authoritarianism.

The Catholic Church was the major parallel institution that competed in representing the "real Italy." Regional bishops met to discuss common problems, and the laity organized into confraternities. These were considered the front line "troops" of the Church, in its attempt to reconquer civil society from the monarchy and from modernism (i.e., secularism). All the groups mentioned in this and the previous paragraph threatened the cohesion of the Kingdom of Italy.

Even more serious were the divisions between northern Italy and the south, or as Italians called it, *il Mezzogiorno* (southern Italy and Sicily). After the turn of the twentieth century, southern Italy was left behind by the more developed and industrialized north. By 1911, per capita income in the Mezzogiorno was about half that of the northern cities. The South became a vital political issue just before WWI and again after WWII. The southern Italians wanted more public works, cheaper credit, relief from land taxes, and they also wanted the cost of education to be absorbed by Rome. Consequently, Italian governments from the pre-WWI premiership of Giovanni Giolitti and from WWII to the present have initiated "low politic" measures to promote economic growth in the backward South, but oftentimes to little avail. The ruling

Giovanni Giolitti

groups in the South opposed many of these measures for southern agricultural development and economic growth because they wanted to keep their stranglehold on their lands and the peasants who worked on them.

Failure in these areas of "low politics," first proposed by Prime Minister Giovanni Giolitti, intensified action in the realm of "high politics." For the Piedmontese and northern leaders, it seemed that the solution to Italy's economic woes before 1914 was to spend more money on weapons and the army, and to turn the army's activities outward. There was a clamor for imperialist adventures abroad, at first in Libya. This desire for warfare led to Italy's participation in WWI on the Allied side. After the war and after Mussolini came to power, it led to Italy's imperialist war in Ethiopia.[6]

Nationalists hoped that these military operations would finally "make Italians" and cement together the congeries of people who lived in the Italian peninsula.[7] To some extent, food rationing, hardships, ensuing complaints, and the army's use of the national language did begin to "make Italians." Nonetheless, the people of Italy remained very divided by the war. To those who had advocated war, "Italy" thereafter meant wartime Italy and patriotism. To those who had not gladly gone to war, "Italy" also meant wartime Italy, but for them it was not a brave and patriotic state but a repressive and reactionary society.

Vittorio Emanuele III

Perhaps the greatest legacy of WWI was psychological and medical. The war left those men who had survived the war utterly exhausted. The impression given by letters written at the time is that of strain, of not being able to cope any more. This feeling was intensified when nearly as many Italians died of the great 1918-1919 influenza as were killed in the Great War. It was this stressed, sick, and exhausted people—still disunited and fractious—who had to deal with the economic crisis of the depression of the 1920s and the rise of Fascism.

---

6. The British Empire attained its worldwide height in 1914. It became a model for Italian imperialist ventures, as it did also for Japan in the Pacific.

7. Japanese imperialism in the Pacific was also a way of "making" Japan in the post-Samurai Period.

Faced with economic and cultural crisis after 1917, the government of Prime Minister Giovanni Giolitti tried the road of "low politics" and made concessions to workers and farmers to buy off and absorb discontent. This only seemed to anger the middle class who did not want to give up any of their perks to those below them. By 1920, Socialists and Catholics threatened the hegemony of the state and its ruling clique. In 1921, Giolitti called for new elections. Once again trying to absorb the complaining elements of society, he offered the parading and marauding Fascists a place in the government. Giolitti's gamble failed. Socialists and Communists gained parliamentary seats, but no government could be formed with these two factions. There were also 37 Fascist parliamentarians elected. This made the formation of a government even more difficult. Giolitti resigned. The swaggering head of the Fascist squads, Benito Mussolini was offered the post of Prime Minister by King Vittorio Emanuele III. Mussolini accepted the offer in October, 1922.

Mussolini Marches on Rome, 1922

PART II

Mussolini and the Fascist Attempt to Make Italy and Italians

In 1924, Fascists killed the Socialist opposition leader, Giacometti Matteotti. *Il Duce* claimed ignorance of the deed, although it is likely that he did order the assassination. The king must have realized this. He could have fired and arrested Mussolini; rather, he decided that the Fascist strong man should stay in power. "High politics" triumphed. Mussolini ruled Italy as a dictator until late July 1943, when the by-then "most hated man in Italy," was removed from the Premiership and arrested as he left the king's residence.

But, as long as he remained in power, Mussolini ruled with a new authoritarianism. What was the appeal of Fascism and Mussolini?

When he came to power, Mussolini promised that the press would be curbed and opposition parties abolished. He also said he would foster a strong state. Therefore, *il Duce* stood on the side of a "high politics" that would unite Italy and Italians. To achieve this, his regime was to be illiberal and authoritarian.

Mussolini followed through on these promises. He used the Prefects of the provinces[8] to control the areas under their control. These Prefects were necessarily members of the Fascist party. But in many ways, control was really shared with the oldest ruling class and not only with the real *Fascisti*. Second, Mussolini used the "*confino*," that is, he ostracized minor anti-Fascists to southern Italy. This had an extraordinary result: for the first time, northern Italian intellectuals directly saw the conditions in the South, and this contributed much to the public awareness of the problem of the South after World War II.[9] Third, between 1925 and 1928, Mussolini neutralized the hardcore provincial Fascists. As he had promised, he no longer allowed the *fasciti* squads carte blanche in their actions, as they had had before 1922.

---

8. Comparable to *Die Gauleiter* in Nazi Germany.

9. A good example of the the *confino* to the South was that of Carlo Levi. He wrote *Cristo si è fermato a Eboli* [*Christ Stopped at Eboli*]. In this work, Levi showed not only the poverty of the *Mezzogiorno*, but also the fact that Christianity itself had not taken hold in areas south of Eboli, like Calabria. The people were still worshipping rocks and trees and not the Christian God.

Mussolini's motto was "Everything within the State, Nothing outside the State, Nothing against the State," clearly a "high politics" attempt at unifying Italy and Italians. His regime was based on the old bureaucratic-military ruling class of the Italian kingdom, and its purpose was to protect the cities from a resurgence of the economic sacrifices put upon them by the "low politics" of Giolitti's government's attempt to ameliorate the lot of the poor.

The Fascist regime promised to restore hard work, patriotism, and morality. The corruption of local Fascist officials went unpunished, for to have punished them would have shown that Fascism had failed to install a moral State. Therefore, at the heart of the Fascist regime, from 1922 to its fall in 1943, was a shell game, a deception which pretended that things worked well, that virtue flourished, and that patriotism triumphed.

Mussolini's one positive achievement was his 1929 Concordat with the Vatican (also known as the Lateran Treaty), whereby Italy recognized the existence of a tiny independent Vatican City state, and the Church recognized the secular Kingdom of Italy's rightful existence. The papacy also promised to be neutral in world affairs.[10] Thus, relations between Church and State were finally normalized, neutralizing one of the institutions that had, since the beginning of the Italian monarchy, threatened the Italian State and its unity.[11]

Other than this treaty, Italy was institutionally little changed by Mussolini. Laws still had to be passed by the Chamber of Deputies. The army and *carabinieri,* the state police, Prefects and courts still ran the State. Above all, Italy was still a monarchy. Yet the loss of the freedom of press, speech, and association under Fascism was not trivial. This price *might* have been seen as worth paying if it had increased law and order, and political stability. But these benefits did not occur under Mussolini's rule either.

---

10. This meant that the officialdom of the Roman Catholic Church never spoke out against the crimes of Fascism, nor did the Pope or the Vatican secretariat of state condemn Mussolini when the Fascist state began implementing laws against Jews. The Church also never condemned the Nazis' heinous crimes against Jews, Gypsies, etc.

11. The situation in France was somewhat similar. After the fall of Napoleon III in January 1873, the Third Republic began to create a secular national school system that pretty much did away with Catholic education. See Eugen Weber, *Peasants into Frenchmen.*

1929 Concordat

Benito Mussolini was a terrible manager. He was impulsive. Suspicious of rivals, he fired most of his competent rivals. It was not a good way to run a country. It was ultimately a lose-lose situation.

After World War II and the fall of the Hitler regime, historians tried to explain how Naziism, with all its horrors, could have come to power in the land of Goethe, Beethoven, and Kant. Historians could also ask the same question about Italy: how did Fascism and Mussolini come to power in the land of Manzoni, Puccini, and Verdi? The answer in both cases is quite similar. The members of both German and Italian governments felt they could let Hitler and Mussolini into the premierships of their states and still be able to control them. But Hitler was able to leverage resentment generated by the Treaty of Versailles' punishment of Germany and the Great Depression, and Mussolini played on the needs of the Italian state as it tried to remain united. Both leaders easily were made heads of their states because the previous parliamentary leadership of both states felt compelled by the coercive tactics of Hitler's Storm Troopers in early 1930s as well as by the Fascist black-shirted squads after Mussolini's march on Rome in October 1922.

It is interesting that Mussolini, even in his post-1938 imperialist, and racist guise, was less warlike than he sounded. He did not immediately join Hitler's war in 1939. He only joined when German victory in Europe seemed assured, and it was in his State's interest to be on the winning side for the division of the spoils of war. Yet his regime had been spawned by World War One; it created war where there was none (Ethiopia); and it ended in the disasters of World War Two. *Il Duce*, as a military leader, was simply a bellicose "man on horseback." He was not long the Prime Minister in formal dinner tails and gloves. But he had no real military acumen either.

When Mussolini's Italy joined the Axis Powers in WWII, it was unprepared in terms of arms and finance to fight as Hitler's partner and equal. Hitler literally had to save Mussolini's army and reputation in Greece; when *il Duce* tried again to help Germany in North Africa, his army's failure contributed to Hitler's army's ultimate fall there. It was clear that Italy was a weak partner, and Hitler had little respect for the Italian dictator. Italian observers realized this, too, and the king and the Vatican began diplomatically to prepare the way for Italy's cessation of the war effort.

By mid-July 1943, the Allies had defeated the vaunted Afrika Korps and they invaded Sicily. Soon the Italian peninsula itself would be invaded. The king prepared a royal coup to overturn his Prime Minister's government. The Fascist Grand Council invited the king to

Benito Mussolini meets with the future King Umberto II in 1944

retake control of the army. On July 25, 1943, Mussolini had an audience with the king. King Vittorio Emanuele III dismissed Mussolini and had him arrested as he left the royal palace. A new, non-Fascist Prime Minister, Pietro Badoglio, was appointed.

German troops rescued Mussolini and he was made Prime Minister of the Republic of Salò in northern Italy, a buttress between Allied troops and Germany. But this republic was a sham. On April 28, 1945, Mussolini, his mistress Claretta Petacci, and two of his fellow ministers were shot by Italian partisans near Lake Como. Their bodies were brought to Milan, and they were hung by their heels in an abandoned service station for the local populace to see and desecrate.

Post-Fascist Italy

Post-Fascist Italy was the opposite of Mussolini's regime. It was a peace-loving, democratic, decentralized State, with guaranteed civil liberties and run by impeccable anti-Fascists. In 1946, by a narrow margin, Italians voted to dismantle the monarchy and to institute a republic. Because he was so closely allied with Mussolini, Vittorio Emanuele III had to abdicate his throne, and his son, Umberto II became king. But since Italians had voted to form a republic, Umberto served as king for only thirty-four days. His abdication marked the end of the Italian monarchy, "high politics," and a victory for "low politics." Italy now was governed by a Chamber of Deputies and a Prime Minister, under a largely ceremo-

Umberto II

nial President. Italy's citizenry became relatively prosperous as a result of the economic miracle in the north of the 1950s and 1960s. But still the South lagged behind.

However, this government of accommodation and prosperity was disliked. People were and still are at the best indifferent to the Republic, when they compare it to their own cities and regions. By the late 1960s economic and social changes raised the question of the legitimacy of the Republic. Its domination by Christian Democrats (Catholic and Centrist) was not popular, and the Italian Communist Party (CPI) wanted a role in the government. Pope John XXIII even spoke, as did other Italians, of a "historic compromise," i.e., an opening to the Left. In the 1970s, Communist mayors came to power in several major cities, and their party played a major role in Italy's parliamentary government as well. These were not USSR-style politicians but progressive leftists, followers of the Neo-Marxist author, Antonio Gramsci (1891–1937), who believed there could be joint rule with politicians of the middle. This recognition of the legitimacy of the political Left was not the only remarkable change in Italy after the 1960s. Electricity and safe water have become the norm throughout most of Italy. Malaria was finally eradicated. Television has made Italy into an increasingly homogenous consumer economy, and Italians became more and more similar to each other in the clothes they wore, the appliances they owned, and the cars they drove. In sum, the problem of "making Italians" seemed increasingly settled.

Reaction to the growing homogeneity of Italian culture and to the dominance of American capitalism led in the mid-to late-1970s to the terrors of the Red Brigades. Their goal was to destabilize the country. Ultimately, Italian terrorism failed to do this, and it likewise failed to make the Italian state oppressively authoritarian or to provoke a coup d'état. Terrorist murders continued into the 1980s, but even when the Red Brigades kidnapped and later killed Aldo Moro, the

The kidnapped Aldo Moro

Republic's longest-serving and only really popular prime minister, in 1978, extreme counter-measures did not ensue.

Terrorism may actually have somewhat strengthened the democratic state and rallied Italians behind their inefficient institutions. Consequently, even after the governments of the clownish and right-wing prime minister Silvio Berlusconi, the Republic of Italy has been until recently, democratic, anti-Fascist, and anti-authoritarian. Its governments and prime ministers change frequently, as they always have since 1946. It is a reliable though economically fragile member of the European Union. Its *lire* and bubblegum and candy currency of the 1960s has been replaced by EU euros, and Italians still think of themselves as Genoese, Sienese, Neapolitans, etc. Tuscan Italian is the national language, but still if you go to Venice, they continue to have a distinct dialect, as do the next towns south of Venice, to say nothing of the *Greki* in Calabria. Italians look to the national capital, Rome, for whatever hobbling attempts at central aid it can give. "High politics" and leaders "on a white horse," like the kings and Mussolini are gone; Berlusconi lingers as an aged leader who still hopes an extremely conservative government will be elected.

Representatives in the Chamber of Deputies, senators in the higher chamber, and ministerial bureaucrats still try to hold the pieces of Italy together. They hope their prime ministerships can last at least two years before they are overturned by "no-confidence" votes. But governments always fail, so that, today, the struggle to "make Italy" and "make Italians" still continues. Silvio Berlusconi, despite his corruption, wanted to become Prime Minister again.[12] His party, Forza Italia (Go Italy), the Northern League, and the Brothers of Italy have joined now to form a Right-Center alliance. The EU Court found Berlusconi guilty of tax fraud, and Berlusconi appealed that ruling. If his appeal had won, he could have run in the election. But, even if his appeal had failed, the Center-Right to Right coalition would have stood and Berlusconi would have remained in the background no matter what happened. Those matters are now moot: Berlusconi died on June 12, 2023, at the age of 86.

Post Scriptum: Who Knows

In Fall 2022 a Fascist government has once again come to power under the leader of the Brothers of Italy, Giorgia Morlani. High politics is once again the order of the day, not the amelioration of the lot of the poor. Will Italy ever be united, and will the peoples of Italy finally think of themselves as Italians? *Chi lo sa?*

---

12. *Reuters News*, September 17, 2017. Also see Jan-Werner Mueller, "United Europe," in *London Review of Books*, 44/21 (November 2, 2022). Berlusconi is quoted as telling his Forza Italia party that he is one of the "five best friends" of Putin, the President of Russia.

Chaptr One Select Bibliography

Giorgio Bessani. *The Garden of the Finzi-Continis.* New York: Harcourt Brace, Jovanovich, 1977.

Richard J. B. Bosworth. *Mussolini.* London: Bloomsbury Academic, 2014.

Carlo Levi. *Christ Stopped at Eboli.* New York: Farrar, Straus and Giroux, 2006.

Denis Mack Smith. *Italy and Its Monarchy.* New Haven, CT: Yale University Press, 1992.

Denis Mack Smith. *Modern Italy: A Political History.* Ann Arbor, MI: University of Michigan Press, 1997.

CHAPTER TWO

Michel Foucault's Confessions of the Flesh and Twentieth-Century French "New History"

"Bon, Donc, Alors,"
Discussions over Coffee, and Movies

I went on my first sabbatical leave to Paris in 1975-1976. My wife Claudia and I lived with her Aunt Régine in her apartment on the corner of the Boulevard Voltaire and the Rue de Charonne in the 11th Arrondissement. It was a working-class neighborhood. I remember that Claudia's aunt said that there were two remarkable things about her apartment and its view overlooking the Boulevard Voltaire. It had its own bathroom and W.C., while other residents of the building had to use the W.C. in the courtyard and had only a sink for a bath; and she had seen from her living-room window the German troops marching on the Boulevard Voltaire into Paris in 1940 and marching out of the city in 1944.

Claudia was a PhD candidate at UC Irvine in modern French literature. She and her friends read and discussed all the major authors and literary critics of the modern period. These included the philosopher-historian Michel Foucault. I understood very little about any of them; I just heard their names again and again. I confess that I felt left out and a bit jealous.

In December 1975, we saw an announcement that Foucault would be giving a series of weekly lectures from December through March. We would have to take the subway at the Rue de Charonne before the sun had risen in order to go to the Collège de France and arrive at the large auditorium where Foucault lectured by 8:00. Claudia initially had to persuade me to accompany her in the cold, dark, early mornings, but I came to see it as a way to enter into her highly intellectualized sphere of friends.

I could see that Foucault was similar to a Rock star. Every week the hall was so full that people were sitting on the floor. Just in front of the podium were placed a dozen or more tape recorders. When Foucault reached the podium, audience members rushed up to turn their recorders on.

Foucault cut a dramatic figure with his smooth shaved head and black turtleneck. Then he'd say, every week, "Bon, donc, alors," "Good, then, so" The words probably meant, "Okay, let's get going. Quiet yourselves down." I'd listen to the lecture. Foucault was never easy to understand, but I had the clear idea that his use of historical evidence wasn't very tight.

He'd finish, put his glasses away, and walk out. (Questions were only allowed after the last lecture. His auditors mostly criticized him then for not being a Marxist. He shrugged and said something like, "You're right." Then he left.)

After each lecture, we exited via the courtyard, and Foucault and his partner, whom I assumed was Daniel Defert, would zoom by on a motorcycle into the city streets to return to their apartment on the Rue de Varenne. Claudia and I always went to a café and we'd always engage in contentious discussions about what Foucault had said. I was like a broken record and said I couldn't understand how he was considered a historian. My wife realized I could not understand such subtleties as his, and said let's just go to a movie.

I always remember "Bon, donc, alors," my confusion, the discussions over coffee, but never what movies we saw.

Years later I delved into all of his books and have come to an understanding of what Foucault was about. It was one of my great joys to introduce my students to his thought. The results of my further study of Foucault since my retirement have become part of Foucault's "gift" that I discuss in the following essay.

Michel Foucault's Confessions of the Flesh and Twentieth-Century French "New History"

"Sin, at the very moment it contravenes God's will or breaks his law, makes an obligation of truth come into effect.... [O]ne must recognize oneself as the author of the committed act and recognize that this act is evil....[A]t the very core of the economy of sin, Christianity placed the duty of truth-telling."

— Michel Foucault

PART I

The Annales Historian Le Roy Ladurie and the Disappearance of Man

The founders of the *Annales* school were the historians Marc Bloch (1886–1944) and Lucien Febvre (1878–1956). In addition to their own books, Bloch and Febvre created the journal, *Annales*, in which the *Annales* School[1] historians have published their research articles.

Before the cost became prohibitive, I used to subscribe to *Annales d'histoire économique et sociale*. By reading its articles, I hoped to understand a great tradition of history. It was important to my development as a historian. One of these historians was Emmanuel Le Roy Ladurie.

Before discussing Michel Foucault, I want to discuss my favorite "New Historian," Le Roy Ladurie (b. 1929) as a comparative tool for

---

1. Most post-1930 French historians belong to this school of history. Based on the beginning of economic history (Karl Marx and Friedrich Engels) in the nineteenth century, the French historians include, beside Bloch, Febvre, and Le Roy Ladurie, Fernand Braudel, Antoine Prost, Robert Muchembled, and a host of others.

understanding Foucault. I think that the most fascinating aspect of Le Roy Ladurie's writing is the gradual disappearance of man from the writing of history. This is somewhat similar to what happens in Michel Foucault's thought, whose ideas on the death of man come, however, from Nietzsche[2] and not from the historical thought of Karl Marx.

Le Roy Ladurie's first important work was *The Peasants of Languedoc.*[3] He began the research for this work with a Marxist interpretation in mind. Marxist history is providential, not in the sense that God is determin-ing the course of history, but simply meaning that a secular history leads to the betterment of human life in society. Le Roy Ladurie's original goal was to show that the growth of capitalist agriculture over the period from the fifteenth to eighteenth cen-turies in the Languedoc region in southwestern France should have led to the improvement of the peas-ants' lives. But, in a moving preface to *The Peasants of Languedoc*, Le Roy Ladurie writes:

Emmanuel Le Roy Ladurie

"Little by little…these happy convictions began to strike me as insufficient if by no means inexact….I had wanted to master a source [the *compoix*, i.e., the survey of land ownership and tax-ation in Languedoc], in order to confirm my youthful [Marxist] convictions. [B]ut it was finally this source [that I used for] this time period [1400-1700] that mastered me by imposing its own rhythms, its own chronology, and its own chronological truth. My own early presuppositions had been stimulating, but they were now outmoded [as I saw when studying the *compoix*]."

In other words, Le Roy Ladurie's original theory was destroyed by factual evidence, and it is these facts that "think for themselves" and determine the truth of history. Le Roy Ladurie abandoned his Marxist interpretation and let Languedoc's tax and land-owning records speak

2. Nietzsche 1974: Friedrich Nietzsche. *The Gay Science.* New York: Random. (*Die Fröhliche Wissenschaft,* 1887).

3. Le Roy Ladurie 1976:

for themselves as to what really happened to peasant life during this three-hundred year period. The sources he studied showed that the peasants' fortunes proceeded cyclically rather than in a linear, providential manner, as his original Marxist theory would have required. When he abandoned his original presuppositions, Le Roy Ladurie was able to write accurately about the fortunes of the Languedocian peasants, in other words the truth of what happened to them from the fifteenth to the early eighteenth century. It was a form of economic history, but not one guided by Marxist providential theory.

In more detail, Le Roy Ladurie notes that the peasants' lives started to improve at the beginning of this period: crop production and population grew in the early part of the fifteenth century. But this population growth eventually hampered the well being of the peasants because, no matter how large the growth in crop production, it was not sufficient to feed the ever-increasing number of peasants in southwestern France. These farmers were forced to subdivide their land holds among their male offspring. The result was that male children inherited ever-smaller particles of land. Consequently, individual peasants found their crop production on these particles of farmland insufficient to feed themselves and their families as well as to make money at the market.

Thus, by the turn of the eighteenth century, the peasants were once again as badly off as they had been in the early fifteenth century. There had been a progression of the peasants' lot and then a falling back. Le Roy Ladurie found that the providential, forward-moving progress that Marxian historical theory predicted was completely wrong.

The reader of *The Peasants of Languedoc* also realizes another unexpected aspect to Le Roy Ladurie's book. His tale was told largely without a knowledge or a naming of any individual peasant. In reading *Peasants*, we come to know these fifteenth-to-eighteenth-century peasants and their lives very deeply without needing to know a single one of them. Usually individuals play an important role in history writing (kings, princes, bankers, artists, bakers, thieves, etc.). Yet the successes and failures of these peasants' lives had become completely knowable because of the tax lists. The peasants were anonymous, but that makes no difference for the reader's understanding of the problems that each and every peasant faced.

Emmanuel Le Roy Ladurie's next book was about the men and women living in a heretical community in the French Pyrenees around the turn of the fourteenth century. In this work, these men and women *are* known individually in terms of their names, actions, words, and beliefs. This book is titled *Montaillou: The Promised Land of Error.*[4] The people called themselves Cathars, "the pure ones" and "the good Christians." They were dualists, believing in principles or Gods of Good and Evil. They were originally found in the southern French city of Albi (and therefore they were also called Albigensians), and their adherents spread throughout southern France and in the mountains of northern Italy.[5]

In the early 1300s, Jacques Fournier, Bishop of Pampers (and later, Pope Benedict XII) conducted an inquisition of these people of Montaillou as part of the French king's crusade to eradicate Albigensianism in southwestern France. Under intense questioning, they admitted sexual and other sins but not their beliefs.[6] One womanizing priest, for example, told Fournier about his sexual encounters with several women of Montaillou. One woman confessed that she picked the lice from this priest's hair as a kind of foreplay to making love, and so forth.[7]

Le Roy Ladurie did not evaluate tax record evidence in Montaillou as he had for the great, anonymous story of the Languedocian peasants. Instead, he studied the Vatican Library's copy of Fournier's Register of these interrogations.

This Vatican record satisfied what one might think a modern French *Annaliste* might also be interested in: body language, sexuality, and myth — once the ground work on the economy and population, what Le Roy Ladurie calls the "Ecology of Montaillou" was established.[8] In this first, "ecological"section of *Montaillou*, Le Roy Ladurie discusses

---

4. Le Roy Ladurie 1978.

5. Albigensians also believed that the human race should die out. They therefore did not want to have children because they believed it was a moral evil that would allow the evil material world to continue.

6. Jacques Fournier conducted this inquisition of the people of Montaillou in the early 1300s. They readily admitted their lesser sins, though they were more reluctant to admit the heresy of Catharism. The latter was a mortal sin and could lead to condemnation by the Church and eternity in Hell rather than to a long, if nonetheless limited, period in Purgatory. The latter would have been the consequence of their lesser sins of sexual corruption.

7. Le Roy Ladurie 1979a, 139, 153, and *passim*.

8. Le Roy Ladurie 1979a, Part I. A recent history, Robert Muchembled, *La civilisation des odeurs* (Paris: Les Belles Lettres, 2017) continues this type of Annales history with a cultural history of smells.

the seasonal transhumance of the shepherds with their sheep and goats up into and down out of the neighboring hills, and the sexual unions the shepherds had with their animals in these mountainous regions. The shepherds had long periods away from their wives or other women and had no opportunity for sexual pleasure except with their sheep.

Le Roy Ladurie developed other historical approaches, too. He asserted that the "territory of the historian" is vaster than historical studies such as he had written on the Languedocian peasants and on the Cathars of Montaillou: he wrote on climatology and even suggested that the historian need not study man at all, but rather just climate, weather patterns, tree rings, and even more esoteric and purely "scientific" phenomena.[9] His essays in *The Territory of the Historian* are one aspect of the development of what François Dosse will call the "new history," the full development of the *Annales* School.

Another part of this French "new history," according to Dosse, are the works of Michel Foucault.[10] The latter's work forms the heart of this essay, for I think that Foucault is the culmination of a different kind of historical thinking in the twentieth century, not simply part of the "new history" that Dosse discusses.

PART II

The "New Histories" of Michel Foucault

"God is dead. God remains dead. And we have killed him," said Nietzsche's madman in *The Gay Science*. Enter Michel Foucault, who writes, in a similar way,

> Ought we not rather to give up thinking of man, or, to be more strict, to think of this disappearance of man?[11] Man is an invention of recent date. And one, perhaps nearing its end.[12]

---

9. Le Roy Ladurie 1971.

10. See Dosse 1987. He argues that *Annales* historians and Foucault have both created a "new history." Cf. pp. 180-182.

11. This sounds like Le Roy Ladurie the climatology historian. Perhaps it is such a parallel that caused Dosse to place Foucault with Le Roy Ladurie among the New Historians, as we saw in the previous footnote.

12. Foucault 1973.

With these two statements, God as a ground for moral action ceases to exist either on the metaphysical or on the collective human levels. Although he did away with God, Nietzsche did write about history and saw himself as a philosopher of history.[13] About a century later, Michel Foucault also saw himself as a "certain kind" of historian, unlike any of the traditional sorts of historians, as he clearly says in various places.[14] Foucault believed he was heir to Nietzsche but he also thought that he continued certain trends started by

Friedrich Nietzsche, 1882

the *Annales* historians. But, as we will see toward the end of this chapter, he seemed to have broken from the tradition that "killed" or removed God from history.

To understand the deeper connection between Nietzsche and Foucault, it's necessary to explore further the German philosopher's ideas as they were presented in his work, *On the Advantage and Disadvantage of History for Life*. According to one of Nietzsche's biographers, Walter Kaufman, Nietzsche believed that historical man was necessary in order for societies and governments to function. Historical memory maintained the past and tradition. Unhistorical man was equally important for man's and society's health, Nietzsche thought, because it was only in the act of forgetting that man could forge ahead, act, and create. To these two categories, Nietzsche added a third, "suprahistorical" man. This man looked neither forward nor backward. He instead saw the world finished in every moment and its end attained in each moment. It is man in this category who would look at himself, life, and history as a work of art[15] or, as we will see in Foucault's case, a work of moral self analysis.

---

13. Nietzsche 1980, Part 2 (*Vom Nutzen und Nachteil der Historie für das Leben.*, Part 2).

14. Foucault 1973, pp. xi, xiv. Foucault 1982a, pp. 3-7.

15. Nietzsche 1980. Kaufman 1974: Walter Kaufman. *Nietzsche—Philosopher, Psychologist, Antichrist* (Princeton, NJ: Princeton University Press), 141-8.

PART III

Foucault: From Madness to Sex

How did Foucault understand or want to understand Nietzsche and what lessons might we want to draw from his understanding of the German philosopher?

To those interested in historical theory, both these writers, particularly Foucault, offer profound, existential challenges and difficulties. Paul Veyne, Foucault's friend and faculty colleague in the Collège de France, summed up the problem for Foucault in the following manner:

> "Can we call Foucault a historian? There is no true or false answer to this question, since history itself is one of these false natural objects. [History] is what one makes of it; it ceaselessly changes; it does not offer a secure, everlasting horizon. What Foucault does will be called history, and it will indeed be history, **if** historians seize the **gift** [my emphases] that he gives them and not find it too off-color ['*vert*']."

Veyne's word "*vert*," means green, fresh, or maybe even just picked and untried by most. We will see that six years after Veyne wrote his 1978 essay, a more sexual tone to the word became certainly applicable to one's understanding of Foucault's work. Could this be why historians might refuse his "*gift?*"[16] This is doubtful, since many historians have written about sexual mores since the last quarter of the twentieth century. Or might Foucault's final moral self assessment in *Confessions of the Flesh* finally turn most historians off of Foucault's "gift?"

Nietzsche the philosopher had offered an approach to history that was interesting, but which could be overlooked by practicing historians, if it were not for the fact of Michel Foucault. The latter's histories

---

16. Foucaut's first volume on the *History of Sexuality*, an "Introduction," was published in 1976. Volumes II and III were not published until 1984, just before Foucault died. In these latter two volumes he abandoned the approach he had taken in the first volume. Another volume has been just recently published which I will examine in the next section. At that point *"vert,"* or fresh, new, maybe even untested takes on an entirely surprising meaning. On Veyne's relationship to and conversations with Foucault, see Eribon 1991, 322-3 and Foucault, *L'usage des plaisirs*, 14. *See also* Veyne 1979.

(*Madness and Civilization*; *The Order of Things*; *The Birth of the Clinic*; *I, Pierre Rivière...*; *Discipline and Punish*; and *The History of Sexuality*) offer not just theories but also an historical "gaze" that suffuses his thought.[17] We might even say that Foucault "fulfilled" Nietzsche similarly to the way in which Marx and Engels. had fulfilled Georg Wilhelm Friedrich Hegel.[18]

What makes Foucault so problematic, so "*vert*," to historians? First, as Veyne suggested, it may be his direct challenge to the way history is written as well as his last works that upset traditional historians. Foucault's concept of historical "rupture" or "discontinuity"plays a major role in most of his histories, starting with *Madness and Civilization*. A careful reading of *Madness* reveals that it is really not a narrative history.

In fact, *Madness and Civilization* is a very personal statement. The beginning of the work is suffused with pure rhetoric and not based on pure historical fact and evidence. The medieval ship of fools whereby the insane were separated from landed, sane society takes up the entire first part of the book, up to what Foucault calls the "Great Confinement" of the insane in the seventeenth century. This reveals Foucault's interest in madness as a modern phenomenon. The names of Friedrich Nietzsche, Antonin Artaud, Francisco Goya, the Marquis de Sade, and Sigmund Freud pepper the beginning and the ending of *Madness*. The historicity of the book, after its rhetorical beginning, does not really begin until the seventeenth century "great confinement" of the insane in asylums and continues up to the author's view of himself.

Foucault sees himself in this his first "historical" work and throughout the remainder of his books as an impresario. In *Madness*, he is a master of Unreason and the Mad. In *The Birth of the Prison*, he is an

17. See Martin Jay, *Downcast Eyes: The Denigration of Vision in Twentieth-Century French* Thought (Berkeley, CA; University of California Press, 1993), ch.7 and *passim*. Jay takes up the theme of the "gaze" which Foucault himself uses in various places, particularly in the context of the panopticon-organized prison, hospitals,schools, and the entire society developed in Foucault 1977. Foucault uses "gaze" several times in his last volume of The History of Sexuality, *Confessions of the Flesh*.

18. Hook1994: Sidney Hook, *From Hegel to Marx: Studies in the Intellectual. Development of Karl Marx* (New York: Columbia University Press); McLellan 1969: David McLellan, *The Young Hegelians and Karl Marx* (London; Macmillan). In other words, Foucault started with Nietzsche but finished completely beyond him.

impresario of those whom he says are imprisoned in jails, schools, and hospitals. Finally, he displays himself as a master of those whose sex is silenced.

Foucault attempted suicide on several occasions.[19] These were his own brushes with madness. *Madness* historicized his own experience; *Prisons* historicized his "imprisonment" in the French school system both as a student and then as a professor; and for many years his own homosexuality had been disallowed, too.

Foucault's studies of medicine, prisons, an early nineteenth-century parricide case, sexuality, and language and discourse all reveal a man who studied the past not so much in order to elucidate that past but in order to study the present, the world in which he lived.[20] Some have called Foucault a "historian of the present." I agree, but I would add that he was a historian of the present and of himself. The past was not an evening before the dawn of the present but the present itself. And once he reached his final historical works on Classical and Christian sexuality, *The Use of Pleasure, The Care of the Self*,[21] and *Confessions of the Flesh*, he examined less the past and more his own mind and body through that ancient past, as we will see as we continue.

PART IV

Foucault and the History of Sexuality Reconsidered

Paul Veyne has argued that Foucault was a "warrior in the present." To this warrior, present and past truths are no more than elucidations of currently existing power systems, dominent discourses of the moment. They are part of a struggle between hegemonic, normalizing powers and the individual who has no morality but that which he individually adopts from his own ethical stance. Once the present moment passes, both the individual's ethical position and that of dominating society cease to exist and are replaced by a new moment. There is no "happy end" to this struggle, for the world, reeling from

---

19. Eribon 1991, 26-7. Miller 1993, 54-5.

20. Foucault 1974: Foucault 1977: Foucault 1982b.

21. Foucault 1988a; Foucault 1988b. The French editions of these two books were published in 1984, the year of his death.

one ethically dominant moment to the next, is without finitude.[22] But, in *Confessions of the Flesh* the present moment will be the last moment and that finitude will be leading to another "moment"[23] that truly will be without finitude.

In 1976, Foucault published *The Will to Know*, the first of six volumes that he foresaw as part of a History of Sexuality. These forthcoming volumes were to be as follows:

The Flesh and the Body

The Children's Crusade

The Wife, Mother, and Hysteric Perverts

Population and Race[24]

Only three more books were published in the history of sexuality series, and their titles did not at all relate to what Foucault had projected in 1976. The series now composed only four books:

The Will to Know

The Use of Pleasure

The Care of the Self

Confessions of the Flesh

We don't know why the original volumes and the methodology used in *La volonté de savoir* were jettisoned. But we can infer what was going on in Foucault's mind after 1980.

Just as Nietzsche had been expert on the ancient philosophers, Foucault also endeavored to become an expert in the thought systems of this same period when he wrote the new final three volumes. The Introduction to *The Will to Know* studied the first "rupture" after ancient and medieval times: the repression of sex started, he said in this first volume, with the advent of Capitalism in the eighteenth Century, culminating in the Victorian period, and then again with Freudian thought which was nonetheless unable to open up sexual discourse from its silencing by the bourgeoisie. Thus, when speaking of the twentieth century, Foucault titles this chapter, "We Other Victorians." This was all jettisoned as he continued his History of Sexuality.

22. Veyne 1993, in *Foucault and His Interlocutors,* in Davidson, ed. 1997, 225-233.

23. Here I am using "moment" in the same sense as in J.G.A. Pocock's *The Machiavellian Moment.*

24. As noted on the back cover of *La volonté de savoir.*

In Volumes Two and Three of Foucault's final version of *The History of Sexuality*, he investigates Graeco-Roman and early Christian sexual ethics and family practices. First, Foucault showed how the fourth-century BCE Greek love ethic had allowed love and sexual relationships between men and boys as well as between men and women. Later, under the influence of Stoic thinkers such as Seneca and then the Christian Apostolic Fathers of the first two centuries CE, both pagan and Christian sexual ethics forbade the love of boys and confined sex to monogamous, heterosexual marriages. Then, in *Confessions of the Flesh*, even heterosexual,

Michel Foucalt

married couples had real sexual behavioral restrictions, as one can see in the writings of St. Clement of Alexandria (c. 150 -c. 215 CE) and St. Augustine (354–450 CE). I will elucidate these issues in some detail throughout the rest of the chapter.

Foucault says that the early Church Fathers argued against having sex for pleasure. For example, Clement of Alexandria said that sex should only be between a married man and his wife, and only for the purpose of procreation. Foucault further quotes Clement of Alexandria's teaching that sex should also only occur at certain, appropriate times[25] and never during menses or pregnancy, and only at night. In addition, as Foucault analyses Christian teachings after Clement, he shows that they became even more strict. St. John Chrysostom (d. 407 CE) argued that virginity and continence for both men and women

---

25. See Foucault 2022: Clement of Alexandria, stresses the idea of *kairos*, the right time for sex. For example, Adam and Eve's sin was not sex per se, but as Clement says, it was a sin because the *kairos* was incorrect; it was adolescent sex.

is preferable to marriage, because they allowed the direct unity with Angelic Being and God. Even when married, Chrysostom said, the purpose of marriage was not procreation, as Clement and other earlier Fathers had said, but was a way of preventing men from having fornication with their sisters, with prostitutes, and with servant girls.[26] In the last chapter, Foucault discusses St. Augustine of Hippo. Augustine goes to even greater extremes about sex.

> "What injury to health is not produced by sensual pleasure? Where its action is the most intense, it is most inimical to philosophy. Who can follow a reasoning or think anything at all when under the influence of intense pleasure? The whirlpool of this desire is so great that it strives day and night, without the slightest intermission, so as to arouse our senses that they may be drawn into the depths.

> "What sensible man would not prefer that nature had given us no such pleasures at all?...So possessing indeed is this pleasure, that at the moment in which it is consummated, all mental activity is suspended. What friend of wisdom and holy joys who, being married, would not prefer to beget children without this 'desire' [*libido*]?"

Clement had spoken about the *kairos*, the proper time for sex. Augustine opines that sex endangers truth and philosophy, and is destructive to the male[27]. Augustine also places great emphasis on *libido*, concupiscence. The concupient will of man has existed since Adam and Eve first had sex, he says, and even after baptism and confession the human will remains in this state of moral decay inherited from Adam and Eve's sex.[28]

---

26. John Chrysostom quotes St. Paul and comments on him: men should marry to avoid fornications with prostitutes and servant girls: "[St.] Paul attests to this when he says, 'But to avoid immorality, every man should have his own wife.' He does not say: for the sake of procreation. Again, he asks us to engage in marriage not to father many children....But of these two motives, the most important is that of continence.... [H]e concludes that the latter has only one end: preventing fornication. Thus, at the end of the analysis, procreation has disappeared." Foucault 2022, 209-12.

27. He says nothing about the pleasures women experience in sex or whether they are dangerous to the female personality.

28. There is nothing here about the eating of the tree of knowledge. That tree was really the feelings stirred by the *libido* as "our first parents" passed on overweening desire.

To be saved, Humans need God's free gift of mercy. Augustine adds that it would be far better if the begetting of children did not involve the destructive desire and pleasure of the sexual act, the concupiscence of sex, at all.[29]

What Foucault elucidates, then, is that from the earliest Christian theologians in the first and second centuries to Augustine in the fifth century, there is an intensifying self scrutiny of the sinfulness of intercourse. Foucault had argued in *The Birth of the Prison*[30] that social institutions (churches, prisons, schools, hospitals) are all-seeing, panopticons, that watch every prisoner, every patient, every student, every teacher or professor. Now, he shows that, from Stoic philosophers like Seneca and early Christian

Saint Augustine
by Philippe de Champaigne, 1650

moralists, to Augustine, individuals have to scrutinize themselves: they have to watch, examine, their every action and thought, especially those which would endanger monastic virginity and continence among the married, as well as the inherent corruption of the human will.

The main point in the *Confessions of the Flesh* is that men who once could love each other were forbidden by Stoic and Christian philosophers and theologians to have same-sex relations; then even male-female marriages had to be examined lest intercourse took place at improper times; then even worse, the male's intercourse with his wife was so pleasurable that his superiority as a thinking being collapsed.[31]

---

29. Foucault 2022, Part 3.

30. Foucault 1977,

31. Foucault 2022: John Chrysostom also makes clear that the male is superior to the female, that he should teach his wife how to act, and that she be given specific household and child care duties, while her husband went out into the public forum.

In studying these ancient pagan and Christian sources, Michel Foucault searched for his own "inner experience" in thought and action and strove to historicize his experience and soul. Men do not exist outside time and the individual who defines his own nature. Foucault wanted to study the history of sexuality, especially in the last volume, to guide himself, a gay man, on a path of "recourse to God." Let us further examine why.

PART V

Where Did Foucault Appear to Be Going before the publication of Confessions of the Flesh?

James Miller's excellent biography of Foucault argues that Foucault's goal was to attain the "limit experience." Miller says that Foucault certainly did this physically in the San Francisco bath houses in the early 1980s and by experimenting with LSD in Death Valley. But he also tried to reach (and succeeded in doing so) the "limit experience" in history. His "limit experience" was to make the study of the past ultimately the study of himself, of his own values versus those of society and even those of the general historical profession. In each generation of historians, individual historians have to ask "new" questions that are meaningful to them and their age. Foucault lived at the dawn of the LBGTQ Age, at the moment when gay men were dying of AIDS and when the general society thought (wrongly) of AIDS as a "Gay cancer."[32]

It is not surprising, then, that Foucault's research for new answers to his new questions attained a high level of narcissism. For him the study of history penultimately became an act of individual passion and pleasure just as his visits to the bath houses and his use of LSD in Death Valley had been. His history becomes asocial and apolitical so that only the self remains as the subject. This is what can make Foucault's historiographical "gift" so acerbic and off-color to historians. It criticizes traditional intellectual and materialistic history and valorises the self-centeredness of history.

---

32. See Shilts 2007.

We can thereby see how Foucault drew his ideas from Nietzsche's critique of "historical" man and his call for "unhistorical" man. We can see that Foucault's penultimate book before his death, *The Care of the Self,* was an important step for Foucault from "unhistorical" happiness to the "supra-historical" self as a work of art, self-indulging, as I have said, while he was a visiting professor at UC Berkeley, and even in his final paroxysms as life expired from his body in the agony caused by AIDS.[33] All this was penultimate.

Foucault's ultimate "becoming free" in *Confessions* may have been because Foucault was indeed getting close to what Roland Barthes termed "writing zero degree," that is de-anthropomorphic, colorless writing.[34] Man and metaphor are gone.

Where was Foucault heading? Some indication may be seen in the interview he gave to the Gay and Lesbian magazine, *The Advocate*[35]. There, he spoke of "creating a Gay life without limits, " of "pleasure disassociated from sex," of sadomasochism "whose practices insist that we can produce pleasure with very odd things, very strange parts of our bodies." Foucault further indicates that he was not only personally but also intellectually interested in the history of homosexual and sado-masochistic subcultures and the history of "friendship," redefined after the sixteenth century when, he said, male friendship was prohibited.

This is the very point of "rupture" in *Madness and Civilization* where Foucault saw the prohibition of delirium and madness as well. He clearly saw his sexual definition and madness-happiness as the sum-mation of his own being and his ability to stand separately from the rules of a "herd" society, to use Nietzsche's term. But the real *ultimate* for Foucault was his own self realization or confession as he prepared to meet his Maker.[36]

---

33. Shilts 2007.

34. Barthes 1968, xvi. It is true that Foucault's writing in the last three *History of Sexuality* volumes are plainer, less encumbered with the rhetorical flourishes of all his previous books.

35. Gallagher and Wilson August 1984. The interview with Foucault took place in 1982.

36. Foucault had said he did not believe in God. I think this changed at Saulchoir and when he wrote *Confessions of the Flesh.*

The Last, Other Foucault

Foucault wrote in his will that all remaining writings that had not been published by the time of his death should remain unpublished. However, his nephew allowed his uncle's *Confessions of the Flesh* to be published in 2018[37].
Confessions is an overwhelming book. After he had written previous books on the history of sexuality which criticized sexuality in the Victorian age, and another that marveled at the ability of the ancient Greeks to enjoy male to male sex[38], *Confessions* examines in

Michel Foucalt

great detail, as we have seen above, and without the kind of criticisms of society and its discourses found in his other histories, the ideas on sex, baptism, penance, concupiscence of the Apostolic and the Patristic Fathers from the first to the fifth century. *Confessions of the Flesh* is replete with the commentaries and homilies of those who formed the Christian views on sex, marriage, and becoming close to God both in the monastic and secular life.[39]

This book is a study of sin, forgiveness, and obedience. It is as if Foucault wanted to study the most serious of concupiscent sins, sex, the taking on of public penance by the sinner with the permission of the priest or bishop, and the obedience of the sinner to his superior, even in the monasteries.

After pages upon pages discussing these Fathers' rules and admonitions about sex, confession, penance, obedience, and their most extreme statements about both the virginal monastic life and the continent

---

37. Foucault 2022: French edition's title is *Les aveux de la chair*.

38. For the Greeks, this meant the love of an older (wiser?) man for a young man, even a teenager. The younger man would eventually assume the older role and would, in his turn, have a younger male sexual partner.

39. The Apostolic and Patristic Fathers that Foucault quotes in great detail are Clement of Alexandria, *The Shepherd* of Hermas, St. Hilary, St. Jerome, St. Ambrose, St. John Cassian, St. John Chrysostom, and St. Augustine.

married life, Foucault concludes *Confessions* by saying that these ideas have formed Western morality even to the present day. He does not criticize this morality. He seems to accept it as good.

Foucault researched and wrote this book at the Dominican Bibliothèque du Saulchoir. I think that this place was not just easier to work in than the Bibliothèque Nationale, as he said. Sometime after 1980, Foucault realized he had AIDS or at least knew he was seriously ill, and probably confessed his sexual sins to Brother Michel Albaric, the head librarian at Saulchoir and a Dominican Brother, and there he began studying these harsh teachings on sin, penance, and obedience of the Early Church, as well as on the moral decay of the concupiscent human will. Only God could take, *sub gratia sua*, humans into heaven. Foucault's enterprise in this last book may well be seen as his way of realizing his own moral decay,[40] and doing penance while he still had time. To achieve the forgiveness of sin, Foucault had to study and accept his sins and, as he put it, "the recourse to God." This may explain why he did not want *Confessions* to be published. It was, in a very real sense, his confession. The Catholic Confessional is private, never allowed to be made public. Because of his nephew's decision to allow his confession to be published, we have Foucault's last thoughts on how he had transgressed, for this book is a symbol of his own self-scrutiny about his sinfulness, and how he sought that "recourse to God."[41] In this last period of his life, Foucault seems to have abandoned the Nietzschean "death of God." The man who had once said he did not believe in God, had a Catholic burial, overseen by his personal Shepherd-priest.

---

40. A moral decay which was part of the concupiscence that afflicts all people since the Fall, as Augustine of Hippo described it. See Foucault 2022, Appendix 2.

41. See Macey 1995, pp 417-8, where Macey quotes Foucault saying he was writing "to become other than he [was]." He wanted to "lose" his " fondness" for himself, to "take care of himself in the right way," to "sacrifice" himself. I believe this is what the study of the Stoics and of the Church Fathers was achieving as he realized the gravity of his illness: the "desexualization" of a gay man who was learning how to confess to himself (and probably to Brother Michel Alberic), to be penitent, and perhaps continent.

The Third Appendix in *Confessions* discusses the role of the Shepherd in Roman and then Christian culture. I think that Brother Michel Alberic became the Shepherd for the salvation care of Foucault. This surmise is strengthened by the fact that when Foucault was buried in the Foucault family plot in Poitiers, Friar Michel gave prayers and spiritual reflections as Foucault was lowered into his grave. He acted as Foucault's priest.

FINIS

The *Annales* journal still publishes articles by historians writing in its tradition. Michel Foucault has been dead for twenty-eight years. No one, to my knowledge, has followed in what might be termed Foucault's final inward-looking, confessional and salvation-seeking way of writing history that we find in the final volume of his History of Sexuality. Regardless of whether François Dosse might have wanted to consider *Confessions of the Flesh* a contribution to the French New History, no one to my knowledge has since written history à la Foucault. A recent book on Foucault has served only to critique and poke fun on his absurdity as a philosopher and historian.[42]

I have read, and constantly rethought Foucault's works ever since I have discussed him in courses at CSULB and, later, at Southern Oregon University. This chapter is an interpretation of how I finally think Michel Foucault turned in his final book to <u>providential</u> history, not Marxian and secular, but religious—with a hope of achieving everlasting salvation. At the end, this historian thought about his own need to confess and to return to faith and salvation. Only Brother Michel Albert knew Foucault's final, unwritten thoughts given in the Last Rites.[43] And that is why he escorted Foucault's body to Poitiers and prayed as it was lowered into the ground.

* *Note Added in Proof:* In a 1968 interview, Foucault hinted at an occupation of his own moral decay and need for confession and penance when he said, "By writing that page, you give yourself, you give your existence, a form of absolution…. That absolution is essential for the day's happiness." (*Speech Begins after Death* [University of Minnesota Press, 2016].) That being said, one could consider the effect that AIDS had on Foucault's state of mind after 1980 and the role played by Father Michel Albert on his writing and intense focus on early Christian thought and its emphasis on the need for confession, penance, and absolution as well as the need for a confession and absolution focused on himself.

---

42. See Mandosio 2010 for what I think is a wrong-headed but thoroughgoing critique of Foucault and a dismissal of his philosophical credentials.

43. There is no record he had the Last Rites (Confession and Extreme Unction), but, again, that would be wholly private, too.

Chapter Two Select Bibliography

Barthes 1968: Roland Barthes. *Writing Degree Zero.* New York: Hill and Wang. (*Le degree zéro de l'écriture,* 1953.)

Bernauer and Rasmussen 1987: James Bernauer and David Rasmussen. *The Final Foucault.* Cambridge, MA: MIT Press.

Burke 1990: Peter Burke. *The French Historical Tradition: The* Annales *School 1929-1989.* Stanford, CA: Stanford University Press.

Burke 2015: Peter Burke. *The French Historical Tradition: The* Annales *School 1929-2014.* Stanford University Press.

Davidson 1997: Arnold I. Davidson, editor. *Foucault and His Interlocutors.* Chicago: University of Chicago Press.

Dosse 1994: François Dosse. *New History in France: The Triumph of the* Annales. Urbana and Chicago, IL: University of Southern Illinois Press.

François Dosse 1987: *L'histoire en miettes: Des "Annales" à la "nouvelle histoire."* Paris: Éditions la Découverte.

Dreyfus and Rabinow 1983: Hubert L. Dreyfus and Paul Rabinow. *Michel Foucault: Beyond Structuralism and Hermeneutics.* Chicago: University of Chicago Press.

Eribon 1991: Didier Eribon. *Michel Foucault.* Cambridge, MA: Harvard University Press.

Foucault 1965: Michel Foucault. *Madness and Civilization in the Age of Reason.* New York, Pantheon. (*L'histoire de la folie,* 1961).

Foucault 1973: *The Order of Things: An Archaeology of the Human Sciences.* New York, Random. (*Les mots et les choses, 1966*).

Foucault 1974: *The Birth of the Clinic: An Archaeology of Medical Perception.* New York, Random (*La naissance de la Clinique, 1963*).

Foucault 1977: *The Birth of the Prison.* New York, Pantheon (*Surveiller et punir,* 1975.)

Foucault 1978: *The History of Sexuality.* Volume 1, *Introduction.* New York, Vintage. (*La volonté de savoir.* L'histoire de la Sexualité. Paris, 1976.)

Foucault 1980: *Power/Knowledge: Selected Interviews and Other Writings.* New York, Pantheon.

Foucault 1982a: *The Archaeology of Knowledge and The Discourse on Language.* New York, Pantheon (*L'archéologie du savoir* and *L'ordre du discours*, 1969 and 1971).

Foucault 1982b: *I, Pierre Rivière, Having Slaughtered My Mother, My Sister, My Brother....* Lincoln, NE, University of Nebraska Press. (*Moi, Pierre Rivière, ayant égorgé ma mère, ma sœur, mon frère...,* 1973.)

Foucault 1988a: *The Use of Pleasure.* Vol. 2 of The History of Sexuality. New York, Random. (*L'usage des plaisirs,* 1984.)

Foucault 1988b: *The Care of the Self.* Vol. 3 of *The History of Sexuality.* New York, Random (*Le souci de soi,* 1984.)

Foucault 2022: *Confessions of the Flesh*, edited by Frédéric Gros. Vol. 4 of *The History of Sexuality.* New York, Pantheon. (*Les aveux de la chair,* 2018.)

Gallagher, Bob and Alexander Wilson 1984. "Michel Foucault, An Interview: Sex, Power and the Politics of Identity." *The Advocate,* no. 400 (Aug. 7), 26-30.

Hook 1994: Sidney Hook, *Hegel and Marx: Studies in the Intellectual Development of Karl Marx.* NewYork, Columbia University Press.

Jay, Martin 1993: *Downcast Eyes. The Denigration of Vision in 20th-Century French Thought.* Berkeley, CA, University of California Press.

Kaufman, Walter 1974: *Nietzsche: Philosopher, Psychologist, Antichrist.* Princeton, NJ, Princeton University Press.

Le Roy Ladurie, Emannuel 1971: *Times of Feast, Times of Famine.* New York, Doubleday. (*L'histoire du climat depuis l'an 1000,* 1967.)

Ladurie 1976: *The Peasants of Languedoc.* Urbana, IL, University of Illinois Press. (*Les Paysans de Languedoc,* 1969.)

Ladurie 1979a: *Montaillou: Promised Land of Error.* New York, Random. (*Montaillou, village occitan de 1294 à 1324,* 1975.)

Ladurie 1979b: *The Territory of the Historian.* Chicago: University of Chicago Press. (*Le territoire de l'historien*)

McLellan 1969: David McLellan. *The Young Hegelians and Karl Marx*. London: Macmillan.

Mandosio 2010: Jean-Marc Mandosio. *Longévité d'une imposture: Michel Foucault*. Paris: Nuisances.

Macey 1995. David Macey. *The Lives of Michel Foucault*. New York: Vintage Books.

Miller 1993: James Miller. *The Passion of Michel Foucault*. New York: Simon and Schuster.

Muchembled 2017: Robert Muchembled. *La civilisation des odeurs*. Paris: Belles Lettres. (*Smells: A Cultural History of Odours in Early Modern Times*. Cambridge, UK. Polity Press, 2020).

Nietzsche 1974: Friedrich Nietzsche. *The Gay Science*. New York: Random. (*Die Fröliche Wissenschaft*, 1887.)

Nietzsche 1980: *On the Advantage and Disadvantage of History*, Part 2 of his *Untimely Meditations*. Indianapolis, IN: Haskett Publishing Co. (*Vom Nutzen und Nachteil der Historie für das Leben*. Part 2.

Shilts 2007: Randy Schilts. *And the Band Played On*. New York City: St. Martin's Press 20th anniversary edition.

Veyne 1979: Paul Veyne. *Comment on écrit l'histoire suivi de révolutionne l'histoire*. Paris: Éditions du Seuil.

Veyne 1993: "The Final Foucault and His Ethics," *Critical Inquiry*, 20 (Autumn), 1-9. (Republished in Davidson 1997.)

CHAPTER THREE

"You Barbarous Dog" and the Left-Handed Hero's Attempt to Reform Roman Catholicism

Prologue

A Hot Date....

A couple of days before I took my doctoral oral exam in March 1968 at Columbia University, my adviser Eugene Rice brought me into his office to discuss how the exam would proceed and what kinds of questions my faculty committee would put to me. I had been reading everything about the Renaissance and Reformation that existed, for month upon month. I felt I was ready for questions in my field of intellectual history and my ancillary field of the economic history of the period.

As I sat in Professor Rice's well-appointed, book-lined office, reflecting on how well prepared I was after months of studying, I was shocked into sobering reality by his first question which was about Frances Yates's *Giordano Bruno and the Hermetic Tradition*.

"**Damnit,**" I mumbled. I realized he asked me this question because Dame Frances had been in New York a couple of months earlier, and she had met with faculty and graduate students at Columbia. He must have remembered I had not been there. **Punishment!**

I had had the audacity to blow off the chance to meet this important and famous scholar, and I had also skipped reading her seminal book on Bruno. I was going on a hot date with the young woman with whom I was spending all my spare time, and an evening in New York City with my girl friend seemed like a lot more fun than sitting around with some English scholar.

So I couldn't answer Gene's practice question, and I sat in embarrassment.

Some years later when I was an Assistant Professor of Renaissance and Reformation history at Cal State Long Beach, I read and reread Yates's Bruno book and had begun translating Bruno's *Cena de le Ceneri*. During a trip to London, I accepted an invitation to visit Miss Yates for tea at her home outside of London. My wife Claudia, my toddler daughter Elisabeth, and I went to Surrey, and we all spent a lovely afternoon getting to know one another. After tea, we stood in her garden and Elisabeth began to pull at the large and abundant chrysanthemums. Miss Yates said, "Dearie, please don't pick the mums. They are hard to grow and I don't want to lose any."

Despite my daughter's mangling of her prized mums, Miss Yates and I maintained a cordial relationship until her death at the age 82 in 1981.

Thus, I came to embrace and deeply delve into the study of the one subject I had neglected in my graduate oral exam preparations. In this way, my path seems to resemble that "left-handed" way described by Bruno in his own endeavors to learn the truth as he saw it and to spread that truth.

"You Barbarous Dog" and the Left-Handed Hero's Attempt to Reform Roman Catholicism

Introduction

Giordano Bruno (1548–1600) was a Dominican friar and philosopher of the late Italian Renaissance. This chapter continues a series of essays I have published which oppose the view of Bruno simply as a philosopher, an adherent of Hermetic spirituality, or a proto-scientist. Bruno was indeed a runaway monk but he wanted to be allowed back into the Dominican religious order so that he could once again receive the holy Eucharist at Holy Mass after his mortal sin of apostasy had been forgiven by the religious authorities. We will see, however, that he also wanted to be permitted to wear the tonsure and robes of the Order, but not have to live in a monastery, and to be recognized as the "*capitano*" of his religion, even above the pope whose religious suzerainty applied only to Roman Catholics on this earth. He believed he was the New Messiah of a new, truly universal religion that promised salvation to the infinite number of beings in the infinite worlds of the infinite universe.

Let us begin with a metaphoric tale of the last supper after Bruno's execution on February 17, 1600.

The End of It All

It was a cold mid-February night in Rome, nine days after the condemnation of Bruno for vehement heresy. Feral dogs roamed the streets looking for places to warm themselves. As one group of dogs neared the Orsini Palace on the edge of the Campo de' Fiori they found a warm spot. Not only was it warm, but there were also pieces of charred bone and meat-scented ash. They settled down to sleep after they had eaten these residues of bone and flesh. They slept calmly for the rest of the night.

The next morning, February 18, the dogs awoke and left, in search of more food. We can imagine street cleaners coming to the spot and sweeping up any remaining ashes and bones, thereby removing the street of the last earthly remains of Giordano Bruno, "philosopher and Heretic."[1]

Thus ended Bruno's eight years of imprisonment in the inquisitorial prisons in Venice and Rome, a period during which the Venetian and Roman inquisitors tried to get him to confess his ecclesiastical and doctrinal errors and heresies. Finally the pope told the Roman inquisitors not to torture Bruno to get a confession, but just to get this seemingly endless trial over with, condemn him, and turn him over to the secular authorities to be burned at the stake. They did; he was. And the dogs enjoyed that evening's warm remains in the otherwise cold Campo de' Fiori.

"You Barbarous Dog" and the Poem
That Introduces Bruno's "New Testament"

To the Malcontent

Curse yourself, O barbarous dog,

Who vainly flaunt at me your cudgel and sword.

Beware lest you incense me.

Because you wrongly attack me to my face,

I slash your hide and rip you up,

And if, perchance, my body falls to earth

Your infamy shall be inscribed in [diamond script].[2]

Go not naked to steal honey from the bee;

Nor bite what might be stone or bread;

Go not unshod when sowing thorns.

Do not despise, O fly, the spider's web;

O mouse, despise not frogs;

Flee foxes, O spawn of fowl.

---

1. This is the title of Ingrid D. Rowland's excellent biography of Bruno (Chicago: University of Chicago Press, 2009).

2. "In diamante scriptorium" are Bruno's words. Lerner and I figuratively translated them as "marble" in *The Ash Wednesday Supper*. (Bruno, 1985, hereafter cited as *AWS*.

> *And believe in the Gospel*
> *Which fervently admonishes that*
> *Those who sow the seed of error*
> *Reap from this, our field, Remorse.*[3]

Giordano Bruno fled the Neapolitan Dominican monastery San Domenico Maggiore where he had lived as a monk since the age of seventeen. He wandered throughout Italy for several years, continuing to wear a Dominican tonsure. He went to Bergamo and there he was told that it would be safer for him to dress in secular costume and also to wear a sword. It was in such layman's costume that he went to Geneva where he enrolled in the Calvinist university under his birth name, Filippo Bruno. After quarreling with a leading Calvinist theologian, Bruno left Geneva. As he crossed the Alps, he stayed briefly at a monastery, wearing his Dominican robes. After a short residence in Lyons, he went on to Paris. There, King Henri III appointed him a *lecteur royale.*

In France between 1581 and 1583, Bruno learned about Copernicus's heliocentric theory. He crossed the Channel in 1583 and went to London where he lived at the residence of the French ambassador, the Marquis de Mauvissière. Between then and 1585 he wrote five Italian dialogues that were related to his newly found interest in Copernicus. The first was *La cena de le Ceneri* (*The Ash Wednesday Supper*, 1584), and the last was *De gli eroici furori* (*The Heroic Frenzies*, 1585). These five works were published in London. They were, in addition to two other works, the only books that Bruno wrote in Italian.[4]

Bruno returned to Paris from London in 1585, but he was not welcomed back in the French capital since political and theological moderates no longer dominated the French court.[5] He travelled across Germany, staying a while in Lutheran Wittenberg, and then on to Prague.

---

3. AWS, 65.

4. They were: *La cena de le Ceneri; De la causa, principio, e uno; Lo spaccio de de la bestia trionfante; De l'infinito universo e mondi;* and *De gli eroici furori.* (*The Ash Wednesday Supper, On the Cause, Principle, and One, The Expulsion of the Triumphant Beast, On the Infinite Universe and Worlds, The Heroic Frenzies*). His other two Italian works were *Il candelailo* (*The Candlemaker,* 1582) and *La Cabala del cavallo Pegaseo* (*The Cabala of Pegasus,* 1585).

5. In fact as Yates describes it in GB&HT, he was run out of town!

He finally returned to Italy in 1591 where he found employment with the Venetian nobleman, Zuan Mocenigo. Mocenigo wanted Bruno to teach him the art of memory. By May 1592, Mocenigo began to have doubts about Bruno's ability to teach the memory art and also to suspect his orthodoxy. He brought accusations against him to the Venetian Inquisition. In the following year, the Venetian Inquisitors turned him over to the Roman Inquisition, where he stood trial for another seven years. Bruno began to cave and admit theological errors, but changed his mind and refused to recant. Thus, he was convicted as an obstinate heretic, was turned over to the civil authorities, and was burned at the stake on February 17, 1600, at the age of fifty-two.

After this brief synopsis of Giordano Bruno's career, we can turn our attention to his poem that introduces *The Ash Wednesday Supper* and the four Italian dialogues that follow it, "To the Malcontent."

The Dominicans (*Dominicanes* or Order of Preachers) were known by a play on words as the "*canes Domini*," and their representation as dogs in the later Middle Ages and Renaissance were as ferocious dogs attacking heretics in the service of God. A good example of the portrayal of the Dogs of God can be found in a fresco in the Spanish Chapel in Santa Maria Novella in Florence.

The Church Militant and the Church Triumphant
Fresco by Andrea da Firenze in Santa Maria Novella, Florence, c. 1365 *(detail)*

In this painting, the Dominican Dogs are snarling at and devouring brown canines which represent monks of the Franciscan Order, who were considered to be heretical by the Dominican Order. In other words, Dominican Dogs of the Lord destroyed those whom they viewed as the enemies of the Pope and of the true faith of the Catholic Church.

The Malcontent that the poem discusses is the "barbarous dog," the Dominican Order. Bruno probably used the Spanish word "*perro*" instead of the Italian "*cane*" because he wanted to indicate the Spanish origins of the Order of Preachers whose founder was St. Dominic de Guzmán,[6] as well as to suggest that the Dominicans in their role as defenders of orthodoxy would actually put an end to this new Brunonian heterodoxy, his new idea of the Church, if they were to one day act as judges of Bruno and his ideas.

We know that Bruno returned to Italy so he could make his case with Pope Clement VIII and to convert him to his new supra-Copernican religion.[7] He planned to ask Clement for absolution for his apostasy so that he could, as suggested above, once again receive the Eucharistic host,[8] and to request that he also be allowed to "live in a clerical habit 'outside of religion,'" in other words not to have to return to a Dominican monastery.

The combination of Bruno's post-Copernican and Hermetic philosophy caused him to see himself as a reformist Catholic dissenter who offered a religion to which all could adhere who were antithetical to rival Protestant theologies as well as to strict Roman Catholicism. Bruno's Messianism or, as Dame Frances Yates also called it, "madness," caused him to think that he could be the "*capitano*" of this universal religion that would be consummated once Clement VIII was converted to it.[9]

The poem's first stanza warns the Barbarous Dog, the Dominican Order, not to come after him. If it does, he will be incensed. The second stanza continues with this theme and says that such an attack upon him would be wrong and he would, in return, slash the Dominican dogs'

---

6. The Kingdom of Naples was ruled by the viceroy of the king of Spain, and some Spanish words had infiltrated Neapolitan Italian.

7. Yates, GB&HT, 338-45 discusses how Bruno planned to write a book for presentation to the Pope and his hopes to reform Roman Catholicism, "which pleased him more than any other [religion]." Bruno believed he would be welcomed by Clement VIII (reigned Feb. 2,1592-March 1605) because the Pope had given the contemporary philosopher, Francesco Patrizi a chair in the university. Bruno said that Patrizi believed nothing but philosophy (i.e., he did not believe in religion). Thus, the Pope would welcome him, too.

8. Bruno had twice before requested absolution for his apostasy from the Dominican Order, but had been told such forgiveness could only come from the very highest authority of the Church, i.e., the Pope in Rome.

9. See Gosselin, "A Dominican's Head," 673-8 (cited above); and *Idem*, "Fra Giordano Bruno's Catholic Passion," in *Supplementum Festivum: Studies in Honor of Paul Oskar Kristeller*, James Hankins, John Monfasani, and Frederick Purnell, Jr. Editors (Binghamton, NY, Medieval and Renaissance Texts & Studies, 1987), 537-61.

hide and rip them apart. (In other words he, a Dominican dog himself, would do something like what we saw the Dominican dogs doing to the Franciscan dogs in the fresco in Santa Maria Novella.) The last two verses of this stanza hold out the possibility that members of his former Order might convict him and order his execution: "If perchance my body falls to earth...." Should this happen, Bruno writes, *"Tuo vitupérions è nel diamante scriptorium"*: "Your shame shall be inscribed in diamond script."[10]

The remainder of the poem can be seen as Bruno preaching to his readers, perhaps especially to his already supposed followers, the so-called *Giordanisti*. His words should be seen then as parables, words that can be understood by his disciples, but not by others. The basis for this would be what Jesus says in Matthew 13: 10-17 (which also refers to Isaiah 6: 9-10). In other words, "To the Malcontent" is similar, in brief, poetic form to the Gospel parables, containing words similar to Jesus's admonitions not to give dogs what is holy; not to throw pearls before swine lest they trample them underfoot and turn to attack you. (The pearls and swine conceit is used several times in *The Ash Wednesday Supper*, although not in this poem.) Bruno clearly asserts that the Dominicans are not holy, do not understand his teachings, and are the true heretics.

"Do not despise, fly, the spider's web." This phrase is a symbol for the sun's rays and Bruno's solar religion. The fly is the symbol of evil in general and, in particular, perhaps again of the Dominicans themselves. Do not pursue the frogs, i.e., the false religion, for the third frog in Revelations 16: 13-16 came out of the "mouth of the false prophet."

---

10. AWS, 225. There. Prudenzio says, "And when [the Nolan] must return to his house under a dark sky, if ye care not to have him accompanied by fifty or one hundred torches, which, even though he had to march at midday, would not be lacking were he to die in a Roman Catholic land..." since Bruno had travelled to Roman Catholic France with no great danger before 1584, he must have been thinking of the peril he would be under upon returning to Italy and the Dominicans who ran the Roman Inquisition. It is a sign of Bruno's messianism in 1591 that he finally did dare to return to Italy and to think he could convert the Pope to his reformed, Hermetic Catholicism. Yates, GB&HT, 339, says, "I think the very madness of this plan indicates that Bruno had never thought of himself as an anti-Catholic."

I have changed Gosselin and Lerner's translation "marble" back to Bruno's original "diamond." I think Bruno wanted to indicate that minuscule type font. Paradoxically, the Dominicans' action will be made almost unknowable and the Nolan will be unaffected by his ashes "falling to earth."

"Flee foxes" — the Devil and evil — you "spawn," you mere humans. Bruno is, in short, warning his readers/followers here at the beginning of *The Ash Wednesday Supper* that if they wish to follow Teofilo-the-Nolan-Bruno-"God's beloved,"[11] they must pay heed to these warnings and also watch out for the Dominicans.

On the other hand, *"Al Malcontento"* could be read in still another way. "If by cynical tooth you are pierced, O barbarous dog," might refer to Bruno himself, for, as I have noted above, he often dressed as a Dominican and used the Dominican tonsure after 1578, and he knew that this self-disguising could make his apostasy even more heinous to the Dominican Order and the Dominican-run Holy Inquisition. According to this interpretation, he might have feared that the Nolan-Bruno would be conquered by the cynical pedantry of his foes.

But if Bruno were instead simply referring to the Oxford debate with two dons[12] he presents in *The Ash Wednesday Supper,* he knew in his own authorial mind that he, the Nolan, would defeat those foes, and that there was no chance of his "body fall[ing] to earth" in Oxford. In this case, the poem would be only a piece of rhetorical bravura and hardly worthy of Bruno's sense of mission and seriousness. This counter-argument shows that the interpretation of the poem given in the previous paragraphs is the correct one.

The Left-Handed Messianic Hero

Frances Yates understood that Giordano Bruno was preaching a new religion and she realized that he viewed himself as a new Messiah. She did not identify elements of this poem with reference to the Dominicans. Nor did she suggest that the poem contained images close to Bruno's Dominican training in the Judaeo-Christian scriptures, or that he

---

11. The Ash Wednesday Supper does not mention Bruno's name, even on the title page, but the text says that Teofilo who recounts the story of the dialogue is "closer to me than I am to myself." Teofilo also calls the hero of the dialogue "the Nolan" (Bruno was born in Nola), and "the Nolan philosopher." It is clear that all these names refer to Bruno, indeed are Bruno. And it is also clear that they are "beloved of God," as Teophilus was called in the New Testament. This also connects Bruno to the Messiah, and even gives the suggestion that Bruno saw himself as the "son of God." (Theophilus was the "beloved of God" to whom the Gospel of Luke and the Acts of the Apostles were addressed. (Teofilo is his Italianized name.)

12. Drs. Torquato and Nundinio.

preached them in this poem in a left-handed way for the sake of his religious followers. In fact, Yates did not discuss the image of the left-handed man at all, even though that man appears in the *Cena de le Ceneri* as an engraving of the first letter of Dialogue One. It is not unreasonable to think that Bruno had a direct role in at least choosing if not cutting the engravings in *La cena de le Ceneri*.[13]

The left-handed path and the left-handed man inscribed in the very first letter of Dialogue One are very important for our understanding of

Detail from *Cena de le Ceneri*

Giordano Bruno and the new religion he preached.[14] The left-handed path, in its mythological roots, refers to the "hero journey or quest" whereby the individual (Bruno, in this case) is aiming to develop a thought system that had never before been seen. The right-handed path, which was not Bruno's, does not produce the "hero," but rather people who remain in society's existing culture, i.e., its orthodoxy. The right-handed path would have kept Bruno in his Neapolitan monastery for the entirety of his life, living as one might expect a monk to have lived.

Bruno, whom we can think of as the engraving's left-handed man on the left-handed path, lived a dangerous but creative life. As is clear in the way Bruno talks about the Nolan philosopher (himself), he praised and elevated himself to a position of centrality in his reformed, philosophical religion, and he rejected the authority of the religion in which he had been raised. When he was condemned on February 8, he stood before the Inquisitors and said, "You who condemn me are more afraid than I am who has just been condemned." As he was burned at the stake on the Campo de' Fiori, Bruno submitted himself heroically to the flames, turning his face scornfully away from the Crucifix that the monks of the Order of St. John the Beheaded raised for him to see.[15]

---

13. See AWS, 80. Yates reports that John Wechel, the printer of Bruno's *De triplici minimo et mensura* said that Bruno "cut the figures with his own hand." (Yates, GB&HT, 320.)

14. See Joseph Campbell, *Creative Mythology, Masks of God.* Vol. 4. (New York City: Viking Penguin, 1968). 262-7.

15. Bruno's tongue had been impaled so he would not utter sacrilegious words as

The most intriguing thing about "*Al Malcontento*" is its ending: "And believe in the Gospel which fervently says, 'He who sows the seeds of error shall reap in this our field Remorse.'" The Editors of the Belles Lettres French-Italian edition of Bruno's Italian dialogues come close to the mark in their attempt to understand this phrase and the role of the entire poem in connection to the four other related Italian works.[16] The editors cite three Old Testament passages in reference to the phrase I quoted above. But only one of them says anything like what Bruno's poem has: "Proverbs XXII, 8: "Whosoever sows injustice reaps calamity." The French-Italian edition's editors ignore the fact that Bruno says "Gospel," and well they do, for nowhere in the New Testament is there a statement like this. What, then, can we make of it?

In the Introduction to the Belles Lettres edition of Bruno's *De l'infini, de l'univers, et des mondes*, there is a section titled "L'annonce d'un nouvel Évangile," in which Miguel Angel Granada recognizes that Bruno's philosophy of an infinite universe with infinite numbers of worlds and inhabitants has an "evangelical dimension" that is anti-Aristotelian and also antagonistic to Christianity (because of the "solidarity of Christ with Aristotle [in Scholastic philosophy] at this historical moment.") Granada is correct in saying that Bruno is opposed to Christian Aristotelianism. But the Nolan philosopher's Messianism is for his new supra-Copernican[17] religion and, I would argue, for a Catholicism reformed along Brunonian lines.

The Belles Lettres editors of Bruno's last Italian dialogue, *Des fureurs héoriques,* argue that Bruno had a clear design for his Italian dialogues from the very first, in other words that he knew what he was going to write in the four dialogues subsequent to *The Ash Wednesday Supper,* ending with *The Heroic Frenzies.* Accordingly, we can construe "To the Malcontent" not only as the poetic introduction to *The Ash Wednesday Supper* but also as the introduction to all five of the related Italian dialogues that Bruno wrote and published in England. Bruno's "Gospel"

---

the flames engulfed his body. The point of the Crucifix was to allow him one last chance to return to orthodox belief. He could thereby have avoided condemnation to Hell and gone instead to Purgatory and, eventually, to Heaven. But the Hero maintained the left-handed path until he was fully reduced to ashes.

16. Oeuvres Complètes de Giordano Bruno (Paris, Belles Lettres), Vol. IV, xxi-xxx; and Vol. VII, xlix-liv.

17. Supra-Copernican because Bruno believed in an infinite universe.

is not the Gospel found in the New Testament. Bruno's is the testament of his religion based on the infinity of the universe and multiplicity of worlds and people. It is appropriate for Bruno to have alluded to a passage in Proverbs since The Old Testament is, once he excluded the teaching magisterium of the Roman Catholic Church, the predecessor of his new Evangelism. (The New Testament centered on Jesus Christ obviously could not play a role once Bruno assumed the role of the Messiah.)[18]

We can therefore understand the manner in which Bruno discusses the Old Testament at the beginning of Dialogue Four of the *Ash Wednesday Supper*. He saw the Jewish Scriptures as providing the Mosaic Law for maintaining the good order of society. It has not been replaced by Jesus's teachings of love and redemption in the New Testament. Bruno's teachings are the real New Testament.

In sum, then, Bruno's proemial poem can be seen as a reference to the Dominican Order, the "Dogs of the Lord," and to the papal master whom it served. Bruno realized they were his enemies once he had become an apostate monk and had begun preaching his new religion publicly in England. He had to steel himself and his *Giordanisti* against them as well as to warn his ecclesiastical enemies. He did so in this powerful and strange poem and the four other Italian dialogues that followed *The Ash Wednesday Supper*.

THE HERO'S END

As I said above, Bruno hoped to convert Clement VIII to his religion of universal infinity and obedience to Bruno's new New Testament's teachings. But Clement deigned not to meet with this new Messiah or to accept his Brunonian religion. Bruno was instead kept in the Roman inquisitorial prison for seven years, during which time the Dominicans engaged him in a kind of intellectual debate between the orthodoxy of the Dominican theologian St. Thomas Aquinas's ideas and the Nolan philosopher's heretical ones. Finally, the long Inquisitorial trial was terminated with a verdict of guilty of obstinate heresy. The Inquisitors

---

18. Bruno would also have to exclude parts of the Old Testament from his new evangel, for example Psalm 18 and Ecclesiastes I: 5-6. These were used to buttress the argument for the Aristotelian-Ptolemaic geocentric cosmology against Copernican heliocentrism.

did the Pope's bidding. A "cynical tooth," like the one in Bruno's proemial poem, ended the debate, but it was the Pope's tooth, not a Dominican's.

And so the hero "fell to earth" as ashes and charred bits. Giordano Bruno had predicted his fate correctly in "To the Malcontent." His earthly remains provided some bit of warmth and sustenance for hungry and tired dogs roaming the Campo de' Fiori on that cold night of February 17, 1600.

And, every year, at least since the time of the nineteenth-century Italian independence movement[19], on the anniversary of Bruno's martyrdom, flowers are placed at the base of his enormous statue in the Campo de' Fiori. The hero still stands!

"Te Barbaro Perro"

Ash Wednesday Supper, Dialogue 3
Bruno's engraving for his "ship experiment"

---

19. See Chapter 1.

Chapter Three Select Bibliography

Alexander, Amir. *Infinitesimal: How a Dangerous Mathematical Theory Shaped the Modern World.* New York: Scientific American/ Farrar, Straus and Giroux, 2014.

Bruno, Giordano. The Ash *Wednesday Supper.* Edward A. Gosselin and Lawrence S. Lerner, Translators and Editors. Toronto, Canada: University of Toronto Press, 1985.

Bruno, Giordano, *La cena de le Ceneri.* In Opere Italiane, ristampa Anastatica delle cinquecentine. Vol. II, 327-466. Leo S. Olschki Editore, 1999.

Bruno, Giordano. *Chandelier.* Les Œuvres Complètes, Vol. I. Paris: Les Belles Lettres, 1993.

Bruno, Giordano. *Le souper des cendres.* Les Œuvres Complètes, Vol. II. Paris: Les Belles Lettres, 1994.

Bruno, Giordano. *De la cause, du principe, et de l'un.* Les Œuvres Complètes, Vol. III. Paris: Les Belles Lettres, 1996.

Bruno, Giordano. *De l'infini, de l'univers et des mondes.* Les Œuvres Complètes, Vol. IV. Paris: Les Belles Lettres, 1995.

Bruno, Giordano. *Expulsion de la bête triomphante.* Les Œuvres Complètes, Vol. V/1. Paris: Les Belles Lettres, 1999.

Bruno, Giordano. *Expulsion de la bête triomphante.* Les Œuvres Complètes, Vol. V/2. Paris: Les Belles Lettres, 1999.

Bruno, Giordano. *Cabale du Cheval Pegaséen.* Les Œuvres Complètes, Vol. VI. Paris: Les Belles Lettres, 1994.

Bruno, Giordano. *Des fureurs héroïques.* Les Œuvres Complètes, Vol. VII. Paris: Les Belles Lettres, 1999.

Bruno, Giordano. *Documents (Le Procès).* Les Œuvres Complètes. Paris: Les Belles Lettres, 2000.

Campbell, Joseph. *Creative Mythology: Masks of God.* Vol. IV. New York: Viking Penguin, 1988.

Cassirer, Ernst. *The Individual and the Cosmos in Renaissance Philosophy.* Philadelphia, PA: University of Pennsylvania Press, 1963. (Reprinted Brooklyn, NY: Angelico Press, 2020.)

Copenhaver, Brian. *Hermetica: The Greek Corpus Hermeticum and the Latin Asclepius in a New English Translation, with Notes and Introduction.* Cambridge, UK: Cambridge University Press, 1995.

Gosselin, Edward A., "A Dominican's Head in Layman's Garb." *The Sixteenth Century Journal,* XXXVIII/3 (Fall 1996).

Gosselin, Edward A. "*Fra* Giordano Bruno's Catholic Passion." In *Supplementum Festivum: Studies in Honor of Paul Oskar Kristeller.* James Hankins, John Monfasani, and Frederick Purnell, Jr., Editors. Binghamton, NY: Medieval and Renaissance Texts and Studies, 1987.

Gosselin, Edward A. "The French Connection." In *Hermeticism and the Renaissance: Intellectual History and the Occult in Early Modern History.* I. Merkel and A. G. Debus, Editors. Washington, DC: The Shakespeare Folger Library, 1988.

Gosselin, Edward A. "Starry Messengers...." Chapter 4 in *Delvings: Italy, Sex, Heresy, Astronomy, and Other Things.* Jacksonville, OR: Weltanschauung Geschichte, 2023.

Gosselin, Edward A. and Lawrence S. Lerner. "Galileo and the Long Shadow of Bruno." *Archives Internationales d'Histoire des Sciences,* XXXV/9 (1975).

Kristeller, Paul Oskar. "Bruno." In *Eight Philosophers of the Italian Renaissance.* Stanford, CA: Stanford University Press, 1964.

Lerner, Lawrence S. and Edward A. Gosselin. "Giordano Bruno." *Scientific American, 228/4 (April, 1973).*

Rowland, Ingrid D. *Giordano Bruno: Philosopher, Heretic.* New York: Farrar, Straus and Giroux, 2008.

Schmidt, Charles B. "The Perennial Philosophy from Agostino Steuco to Leibniz. *Journal of the History of Ideas,* xxvii (1966), 505-32.

Vesel, Matjaz and Robert Westman. "Debate." *Isis,* 108/3 (Sept. 2017), 657-8.

Walker, D. P. *The Ancient Theology: Studies in Christian Platonism from the Fifteenth to the Eighteenth Century.* Ithaca, NY: Cornell University Press, 1972.

Yates, Frances A. *Giordano Bruno and the Hermetic Tradition.* Chicago: University of Chicago Press, 1964.

Yates, Frances A. *The Art of Memory.* Chicago: University of Chicago Press (reprint edition), 2001.

CHAPTER FOUR

Starry Messengers: From the Scribes of Uruk and Babylon to the Michelson-Morley Experiment and Einstein's Theory of Special Relativity

Prologue

The Danish Expedition, Ancient "Scratchings," and Exact Mathematical Astronomy

Europeans had been long interested in the Middle East. Religious explorers wanted to investigate the region that surrounded the Holy Land — not just the land of the ancient Hebrews but also that of the ancient Assyrians, Sumerians, and Egyptians whose leaders figured as enemies of the Hebrew peoples. Some had gone to the regions and come across friezes erected in honor of these ancient kings. They saw writings on walls and on tablets, but they could not read them. They looked like hen scratchings. Yet once these "scratchings" were able to be understood and read, the first great literary work, *The Epic of Gilgamesh*, and the first works of exact astronomical science became known to modern Western people. In terms of this chapter, the first scientific revolution was discovered.

Frederick V, King of Denmark, commissioned a scientific expedition to the Middle East to investigate the ancient cities and their remnants. The expedition left by ship in the winter of 1861. Their goal was Turkey, Egypt, and Yemen, known for centuries as *Arabia Felix,* "Fortunate Arabia."[1]

The expedition was made up of six men: two Danes, two Germans, a Swede, and a man servant. They were scholars: a botanist, a doctor, a philologist, an astronomer, and an artist. Their goal was to create a complete picture of this land that up to this point was almost unknown to Europeans.

Things did not go well. The five scholars of the expedition very quickly hated each other. They eventually even threatened to kill one another. This didn't happen, but all but one of them died of disease during the expedition. Finally, in 1767, Carsten Niebuhr, the lone

---

1. See Hansen 2017, 300-301 on the true meaning of *Arabia Felix."*

remaining member of the expedition, emerged from the Yemenite desert and finally returned to Copenhagen. The king had died in 1766 and his son, Christian VII, was not interested in the expedition or the drawings of cities and plant life, or the cuneiform alphabet that Niebuhr had sent back. So all the expedition's monumental work was stuffed away in a Copenhagen library unexamined for years.

Niebuhr had copied cuneiform letters from the ruins of the ancient city of Persepolis. He attempted to create from them what he thought (quite correctly) was the cuneiform alphabet, which people had seen as hen scratchings years before.

Niebuhr was not the last European to be interested in deciphering cuneiform and trying eventually successfully to learn its grammar and then its mathematics.

In 1827, Henry Creswicke Rawlinson went to India as a cadet for the British East India Company. He went to Iran with other members of the Company and became interested in Persian antiquities. After two years he was able to copy and translate two paragraphs from a cuneiform wall in honor of the Persian Emperor, Darius I, at Behistun*. In 1850, he succeeded in understanding the cuneiform grammar, and he published *Persian Cuneiform Inscription at Behistun*.

Europeans going to the Middle East thereafter came back with ship loads of cuneiform tablets. The number of tablets in libraries in Istanbul, Paris, London, and, in the USA, at Yale and the University of Pennsylvania libraries number in the tens of million. Only about one hundred thousand have been examined, copied, and read. But it should be noted that only because of Niebuhr, Rawlinson, and others, can the ancient cuneiform language now be read by Ancient Near East scholars.

Thus, it was the ill-fated Danish Expedition, the British East India's Henry Rawlinson, and twentieth-century Assyriologists like Abraham Sachs and Otto Neugebauer who made it possible that thousands of cuneiform tablets, written by the scribes of Babylon and Uruk, could be identified, copied, and studied.

Once these mathematical tablets were studied, it became clear that exact mathematical astronomy actually existed 2500 years before the European Scientific Revolution of the Seventeenth Century.

*Northwestern Iran

Starry Messengers: From the Scribes of Uruk and Babylon to the Michelson-Morley Experiment and Einstein's Theory of Special Relativity

Die Naturwissenschaft steckt im Detail[2]

Introduction

When the ordinary person thinks about science, he or she probably has only the dimmest understanding of what it is or how it came to be. Most could probably conjure the names of Galileo and Newton if they were asked how science began, but not know too much beyond these names. I taught the history of science for thirty years, and I know that Galileo and Newton are indeed really the starting points for most people who think about the history of science.

I want to provide a longitudinal understanding of how science began and developed, especially exact mathematical astronomical science. There was astronomical science long before the sixteenth and seventeenth centuries, and often it was quite accurate. Therefore, it can truly be said that mathematical and observational astronomy has been ongoing for some 2500 years. And, as we will also see, the science in the so-called Scientific Revolution of the Seventeenth Century was not always without its spooks, i.e., without what we would today call unscientific or prescientific ideas.

The notion of the Scientific Revolution has to be pushed back at least to the time of the Mesopotamians. This means that, in my view, there was not simply a scientific revolution in the seventeenth century that created modern science. There were a series of scientific revolutions: that

---

2. *Science is in the detail.* Based on "Der liebe Gott steckt im Detail," used by Aby Warburg for his seminar at the University of Hamburg, 1925-6. A French version was also used in the nineteenth century by Gustave Flaubert. Cf. Gombrich 1986, 13-14.

of the Mesopotamian Scribes who turned their eyes to the skies; that of Greek thinkers from around the time of Plato and Aristotle; that of Ptolemy of Alexandria in the second century CE; that of the medieval Scholastics; and then that of Copernicus in the sixteenth century and his followers a century later. Other scientific revolutions followed in the modern era, that is, in the nineteenth to twenty-first centuries.

This essay will stop with the Michelson-Morley Experiments in 1887-8 and with a nod to Einstein's theory of special relativity in 1905. This seems like a good stopping point for an essay on scientific revolutions for at least two reasons. First, 1888 and 1905 brought to an end the remnants of Isaac Newton's spookish idea of the Aether that was a major component of his thought; and, second, it is the beginning of an entirely new era in astronomy.[3]

The First Scientific Revolution?

Excursus 1

The Babylonian section uses three dating systems. Two are familiar to all: BCE is what we used to call BC, and CE is the former AD. The third dating system used in the section on Babylonian astronomy is SE. It means "Seleucid Era." Seleucid Era dating was used by the Hellenistic Babylonians, Assyrians, Sumerians, and Jews who lived within the Kingdom of Seleucus, (The Seleucid Kingdom stretched from Thrace in Europe to the border of India.) Seleucus was a general in Alexander the Great's army. After Alexander's death in 323 BCE and after Seleucus's subsequent period of imprisonment in Egypt, Seleucus reconquered Babylon in 312 BCE, and so 311–310 BCE was the year 1 in the Seleucid calendar. The year 113 SE in Table 1, below, is the same as 199 BCE.[4]

In addition, Figure 1 below shows that the Babylonians had "hollow months" and "full months." They followed a lunar calendar, but their hollow months and full months were similar to our twenty-eight day February and our thirty and thirty-one day months.

---

3. This chapter contains some sections that I call *Excursi*. They indicate somewhat deeper explanations of issues being discussed.

4. Interestingly, the Seleucid dating system was still used as late as the sixth century CE by Syrians and in the fourteenth century CE on Nestorian Christian tombstones in Asia Minor.

LET'S BEGIN WITH BABYLONIAN CULTURE AND SCIENCE:

The Mesopotamian version of modern America's STEM!

The earliest men were nomads, moving from place to place to find food. Around the fourth millennium BCE, some nomads began to settle in the region between today's Syria and Kuwait, most especially along the Tigris and Euphrates Rivers. There, they founded cities, the most notable of which were Babylon and Uruk. They also developed a settled agriculture, growing crops around their cities. The peoples who lived along the Tigris and Euphrates Rivers go by several names: Sumerians, Mesopotamians, Assyrians, Babylonians, and Akkadians. I will use the terms Mesopotamians and Babylonians henceforth.

These Mesopotamians developed an alphabet, a literature, and also an arithmetic mathematics. Their alphabet began in a pictographic form. We ourselves use pictographic language even today. For example, we may have a bottle with the image of a skull and crossbones on the label, giving the clear message, "if you drink the contents you will die." So, the Mesopotamians might have drawn a foot. It might mean a foot or, along with a crude drawing of a human, in could mean "walk." A star might mean just that, or it could mean the sky or the heavens where the gods live.

This pictographic drawing eventually developed into an alphabet by which more complex ideas could be expressed. In the same way, arithmetic symbols could be expressed: four strokes or lines could mean our number 4. One stroke with a slight space following it and then four strokes could mean 64. The Babylonians' mathematics was based on the **sexagesimal system**, the base-sixty system: every total of 60 strokes equaled 1. (We still use this base-sixty system today in our time keeping: 60 second equals 1 minute, and 60 minutes equal 1 hour.) Two strokes followed by four strokes equaled twenty-four hours, or one day. In other words single strokes could mean 1, or 10, or twenty-four, which also meant one day. The context of the strokes determined the meaning.

The writing and language used in ancient Mesopotamia is called cuneiform. The oldest piece of literature in the world comes from this

Babylonian form of writing: *The Epic of Gilgamesh*, written about 2100 BCE, about Gilgamesh, the king of Uruk.

Although our general interest in this chapter relates to a part of the history of science, it would be good to discuss *The Epic of Gilgamesh* briefly in order to show that the ancient Mesopotamians were in the forefront of human thought about the issues of friendship and human existence as well as in the forefront of the development of astronomical science.

Gilgamesh, King of Uruk, was famous as a great builder, for under him the massive walls of the city of Uruk were built. The other main character in this epic was Enkidu. He was a wild man who finally was civilized by a prostitute.

(Interestingly, this fact introduces into Western literature the role of the prostitute who could be a good woman and not just a purveyor of sex.)

Once civilized, Enkidu was sent to the great bastion of civilization, Uruk, where he encountered Gilgamesh. They saw each other as enemies, or at least opponents. And so they struggled with each other. Gilgamesh won this hand-to-hand combat, and they developed an intense friendship. They set off together to the Cedar Forest, where they found and killed Humbaba the Terrible and then they cut down the Sacred Tree.

The goddess Ishtar then made advances to Gilgamesh. He spurned her, and to punish him Ishtar killed Enkidu. Gilgamesh was crestfallen at the loss of his friend. As a result, he set off on a long journey to find the secrets of eternal life, not only for himself but also in the hope of bringing Enkidu back to eternal life, too. But he failed. He discovered that there is no such thing as eternal life, and that all humans, including Enkidu and Gilgamesh himself, must eventually die.

Thus, human mortality is the lesson taught to the Mesopotamians by this first of the world's great epics. It rivals the later epics of Homer, as well as all subsequent epics down to Dante's *Divine Comedy*. And it shows that the Babylonians became as literate and thoughtful a people as the later Greeks did as well.

AND NOW THE LATE BABYLONIANS AND THEIR NAKED-EYE ASTRONOMY

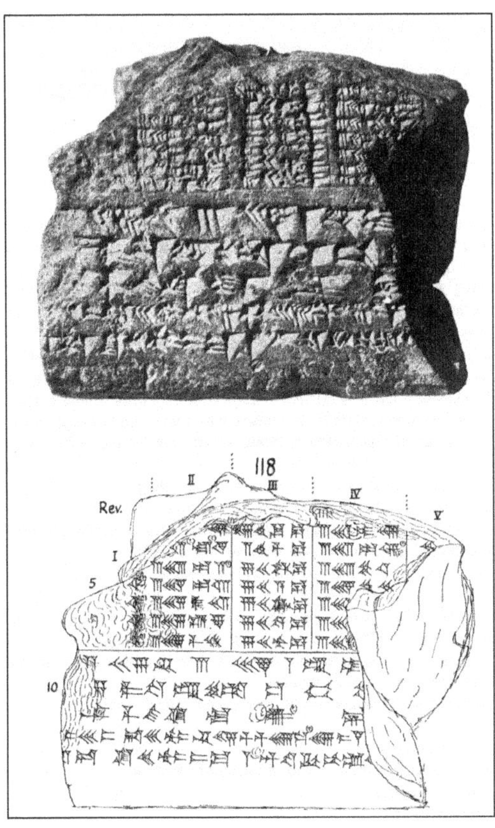

Plate 1

Text 603 with Procedure Text (BM 34371). Above photograph British Museum, below a transcription reproduced from Abraham J. Sachs, Late Babylonian Texts, *No. 118. The upper part is a table for mul-Babbar (the planet Jupiter) for the years 147–218 SE. The transcription below is the Procedure Text explaining the method of calculation used in the table, as will be explained below.*

Perhaps because of the lesson about the impossibility of immortality contained in *The Epic of Gilgamesh*, the priestly scribes in the temples of Babylon and Uruk of the Late Babylonian period turned their attention from the duties of purely priestly religious practice to viewing the sky, and they began to plot the motions of the five planets that can be seen by the unaided eye (Mercury, Venus, Mars, Jupiter, and Saturn). They used the sexagesimal (base-sixty) mathematical system (60 = 1) which all Mesopotamian youngsters learned in school. This system, by the way, continued to be used for astronomical calculations down to the time of Johannes Kepler in the seventeenth century CE. (The base-sixty system is not really foreign to us today, because we still use it for measuring angles, hours, and months.)

The Babylonians computed planetary positions as they saw them (naked-eye astronomy). The planets seemed to pass within the twelve houses of the Zodiac; and the Babylonians kept records of these planetary positions in tablets made of clay, in their ancient language and number system. These tablets have been found in archeological digs, mainly in the ruins of the cities of Uruk and Babylon. They detailed planetary positions (also called ephemerides) and are evidence that the Babylonians developed an exact mathematical astronomy that was precise within six percent of the figures given today in U.S. Naval Records of Planetary Motions.[5]

Planetary movements at first (seventh to fifth centuries BCE) provided the basis for creating omens predicting political, commercial, and agricultural outcomes as well as for explanations of events that had already occurred. For example, one tablet's so-called omen wrote:

> "If mul-babbar [Jupiter] becomes visible in the eighth month,
> one king will send hostile messages to another, business will
> diminish, and physicians should not try to heal."[6]

This use of omens or prediction calendars lasted in Europe into the eighteenth century CE. The main purpose was, as it had been for the Babylonians, to register pagan gods,' now Christian saints,' days so that proper prayers and offerings might be made to these gods/saints at the appropriate times. Horoscopic prediction was considered a science as late as the nineteenth century, when at last it came to be viewed as a pseudo-science for the predictions of wealth, love, and health. Instead of going to a learned astrologer (the earliest star-gazer), one only had,

---

5. Gosselin 1985, Notes. Planetary stationary points are when a planet's apparent motion stops or apparently changes position. The ephemeris of mul-babbar that we will be discussing details the first time that planet seems to stop with respect to the stars each month or so in its procession through the zodiac.

6. Swerdlow 1998, 9.

and in some cases still has, to read the horoscopes found online in many newspapers.

By the fourth century BCE, the priests of the temple of Marduk in Babylon began to plot the synodic positions of the planets over months and years. Astrologer-priests had become astronomer-priests. These Scribes no longer plotted planetary positions for "omens," but more and more for the sole purpose of doing exact arithmetic astronomy, a way to determine the longitudes of the planets as they seemingly passed through the twelve houses of the Zodiac, each one 30° in distance from entering a Zodiacal house to exiting it and entering into the next house. It is this Scribal astronomy that was the first precise scientific system, and it was similar in almost every way to the goals and methods of modern science. The scribes' mathematical and technical astronomy was indeed far superior in its mathematical technicality to the Pre-Socratics and, later, even Aristotle , whom "most historians and philosophers today extoll because these modern scholars are often without comprehension" of the rigorous mathematical system that the Babylonian Scribes had created.[7]

Using what historians of science such as Otto Neugebauer have called System A, the Scribes charted each of the visible planets: *gu4-tu* [Mercury], *d'il bat* [Venus], *sal-bat-a-nu* [Mars], *mul-babbar* [Jupiter], and *ginna* [Saturn], plotting their synodic stations, that is, where they stopped as they seemed to follow the path of the Sun which is known as the ecliptic.

This astronomy was, then, an ecliptic-coordinate system and, as Yale's Asger Aaboe pointed out, "It is still used [today] for problems involving sun, moon, and planets." They are either on the ecliptic[8] (i.e., the Sun itself) or near it (i.e., the moon and the planets). Their celestial latitudes are small — Venus, which has the largest latitude, is only +10° to -10° from the ecliptic.[9]

Today we count planetary longitudes from 0° to 360°, but the Babylonian Scribes referenced planetary longitudinal positions by the planets' degree positions in the houses of the Zodiac. Thus, the Scribes divided the ecliptic into twelve parts with 30° in each of them.

---

7. Swerdlow 1998, 181.
8. The ecliptic is the path of the Sun.
9. Aaboe 2001, 18.

Accordingly, we have the following chart, in degrees.

Aries	0°-30°	Libra	180°–210°
Taurus	30°-60°	Scorpio	210°–240°
Gemini	60°-90°	Sagittarius	240°–270°
Cancer	90°-120°	Capricorn	270°–300°
Leo	120°-150°	Aquarius	300°–330°
Virgo	150°–180°	Pisces	330°–360°

If an ephemeris[10] placed a planet at Libra 12°, in modern notation that would be 192°. If the position of the planet in the Zodiac increases in a following month or year, then the planet moved directly, or forward; if it decreases, according to the ephemeris, then that indicates a retrograde motion. (This way of indicating forward or backward motion is, as we will see, what Ptolemy of Alexandria later achieved by the use of planetary epicycles within the spheres of the planets.) In the ephemeris for mul-babbar (a section of which is given below), we are told at its end what procedure was used in creating the mathematical record of mul-babbar's position:

> "**From Gemini 25° to Scorpio 30°.** Whatever exceeds Scorpio 30°, multiply by 1;12 and add it to Scorpio 30°.
> "**From Scorpio 30° to Gemini 25°.** Whatever exceeds Gemini 25°, multiply it by 0;50 and add it to Gemini 25°."

As can be seen, then, the ecliptic is divided into a fast and a slow arc. Inside these arcs, the synodic phenomenon progresses in steps of 36° and 30°. Crossing a boundary of the arcs, the amount mul-babbar extends into the new region is multiplied by 0;50 or 1;12 (sexagesimal figures). As fractions, these are 5/6 and 6/5, or 30:36 and 36:30. Using this rule, the ephemeris can be extended forward or backward in time as long as you want or, to be more historically accurate, so long as the Babylonian Scribes wanted and the size of the clay tablet allowed.[11]

Even more interesting is the fact that if the Scribes knew Jupiter's longitude and the time it was at a first stationary point through one single observation, the procedure text colophon quoted above enabled them to determine where and when it would next be at a first stationary

---

10. Singular form of ephemerides table giving planetry positions.
11. Gosselin 1985, Notes.

point in the future, or when and where it had been at a previous first stationary point in the past months and years. In this way, the Babylonian scribal astronomers could create accurate planetary ephemerides for all the then-known planets for spans of thirty years or more, using these arithmetic calculations.

Finally, the Scribes were able to compute a precise return of Jupiter to the same longitude after a period of 427 years. This is extraordinary, for these Scribes in their temples gazing at the skies could achieve what today's astrophysicists can also do with sophisticated telescopes and the calculus. For example, starting at Aries 8;6, after 391 synodic periods of *mul-babbar* (in this case first stationary points), add the planet's 36 revolutions during this period, and you have 427 years when the first stationary point of Jupiter will again be at Aries 8;6.[12]

While System A's arithmetic procedures should display all the synodic positions as the planets passed through the Zodiac along narrow latitudes from the ecliptic, the Late Babylonian astronomers also used a System B which was not as accurate as System A, in that it did not compute longitudinal positions along the course of the houses of the Zodiac, but rather the number of particular synodic events (e.g., first stationary points) that occurred within a period of time, once the place of the first event was known.[13] Both Systems A and B were used simultaneously in Babylon and Uruk.[14] Thus, it's clear that Babylonian arithmetic astronomy was fully developed by no later than 300 BCE. We should note, along with Asger Aaboe, that Babylonian astronomy "is entirely arithmetical in character or, in negative terms, there is no trace of geometric models like the ones we have been accustomed to since the time of the Greek astronomers, Eudoxus (c. 390–c. 337 BCE), Hipparchus of Nicaea (190–120 BCE), and Ptolemy (fl. 150 CE)."[15]

One of the most complete surviving clay-tablet ephemerides is that of the first stationary points of *mul-babbar* (Jupiter). It contains forecasts of all such synodic points between 113 and 173 SE (198–138 BCE)[16]. One part of the original clay tablet is now in the Louvre Museum, Paris,

---

12. Aaboe 2001, 45-46.
13. Swerdlow 1998, 136.
14. Neugebauer 1983, 265-70.
15. Aaboe 2001, 41.
16. See Figure 1.

and the remaining fragment is in Istanbul. We do not know exactly when the naked-eye observation was made, but the entire tablet for past and future years was written on Oct. 5, 118 SE. We for once even know the name of the scribe who wrote the clay tablet, a man named *Ana-ana-uter.* He wrote it in Uruk six years into the sixty years that the ephemeris covers. In other words, his arithmetic acumen allowed him to go forward and backward in assigning Jupiter's position in the sky. Using the rules established in the Colophon quoted above, the Scribe could, with only two mathematical units being known, complete the entire ephemeris. Only one observation of the planet's first stationary point was needed to complete the entire text. That achievement indicates a very sophisticated astronomy.

Both the second century BCE Babylonian astronomers and the seventeenth century CE Galileo used observations and mathematics as the basis for their science because they were "curious," to use the important term employed by Philip Bell in his recent study of the role of "curiosity" in seventeenth-century science.[17] The Babylonian Scribes were extremely curious about the heavens, regardless if they ever used the word "curiosity."

And, whereas the post-350 BCE Scribes had largely jettisoned astrology and omens from their concerns, the "curiosity" centuries later of Galileo did nonetheless allow him to write astrological papers in addition to the famous scientific works that have rightly made him famous.[18]

FIGURE 1: First Stationary Point of *mul-Babbar*, 113-139 SE (198-172 BCE)
Excerpted from my translation of the entire cuneiform ephemeris.

Col. I	Col. II	Col. III	Col. IV
Yr. SE	Tithis***	Month & Day	Zodiacal Position
113**	48;5,10	I 28;41,40	Cap. 8;6
114	48;5,10	II 16:46,50	Aquar. 14;6
115*	48;5.10	IV 4;52	Pisces 20;6
116	48;5,10	IV 22;57,10	Aries 26;6
117	48;5,10	VI 2;20	Gemini 2;6

17. Bell 2012.
18. Giglioni 2017, 852.

118*	44;54,10	VII 26;56,30	Cancer 5;55
119	42;5.10	VIII 9;1,40	Leo 5;55
120	42;5,10	IV 10;45,40	Virgo 5;55
....	....	....	....
139	48;5,10	IV 10;45,40	Pisces 30;6

115* and 118*: These years contained a month XII.

113**: This year contained a month VI.

Tithis***: The Babylonian lunar calendar had "hollow" and "full" months (29 or 30 days). But for practical calculational purposes, the Scribes, like modern bankers, used a uniform 30-day month. They therefore did not have to determine if it was a hollow or a full month. This 30-day unit is today called by the Sanskrit term "*tithi.*" It could be divided sexagesimally into as many very precise places as the Scribes wanted. (One month = thirty *tithis.*)

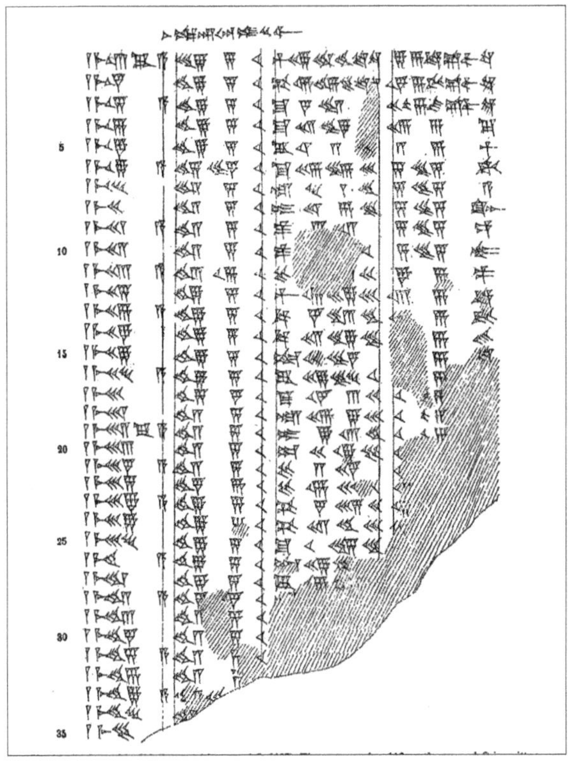

Plate 2

Jupiter table 600 (Louvre Museum AO 6457). Copied by A. Thoreau-Dangin,
Tablettes d'Uruk *(Paris:* Geuthner, 1920), *Plate 50.*

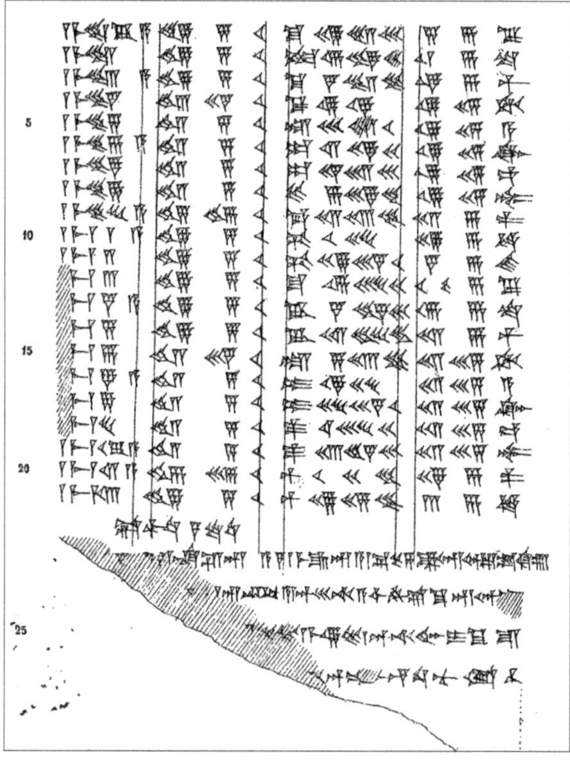

Plate 3

Jupiter Table 600, continued (Istanbul). Ibid., Plate 51.

One further point on Babylonian exact mathematics. Columbia Unversity's Rare Books and Manuscripts Room has a 5"x 3.5" clay tablet, known as Plimpton 322. This cuneiform tablet was discovered in Larsa, a Sumerian city in the Fertile Crescent, in 1922. It is about 3700 years old, and on it are 60 numerals. According to Otto Neugebauer, they are Pythagorean triples, i.e., they are the classic right triangle equation $(A^2 + B^2 = C^2)$. This shows that 3700 years ago (ca. 1678 BCE), the Scribes understood the Pythagorean right triangle formula eleven hundred years before Pythagoras lived (ca. 570 BCE–ca. 495 BCE). Two Australian scholars have also argued that this tablet "used a kind of trigonometry based on ratios, not angles and circles." This predates Hipparchus (190 BCE–120 BC), usually called the "father of trigonometry" by about 1500 years.[19]

---

19. "Babylon Revisited." Columbia Magazine. Winter 2017.

On the other hand, when Euclid wrote his theorem on the Pythagorean principle (*Elements*, Bk. I, theorem 47), he did not use numbers to prove this or any other of his theorems. He literally built squares on each side of the right triangle and proved that the sum of the areas of the actual squares of each of the two sides (A and B) equaled the area of the square built on the hypotenuse (C). The Babylonian Scribes, on the other hand, did use mathematics (numbers). "My God, the Babylonian Scribes were smart," as Noel Swerdlow said.

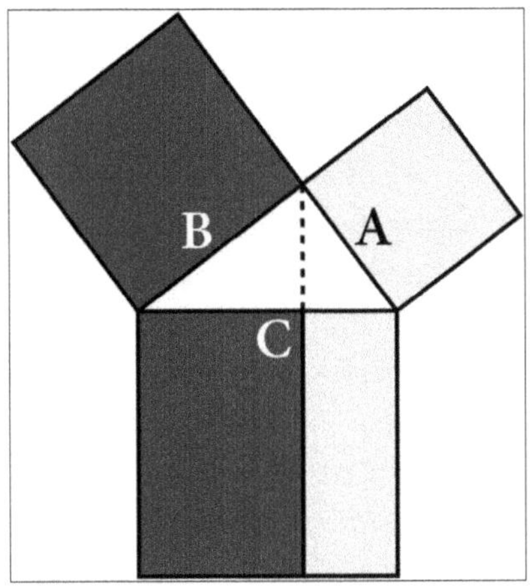

FIGURE 2: Euclid did not use the algebraic formulation we use to prove the construction ($A^2 + B^2 = C^2$). He literally built the squares in each side.

HOW DID THE GREEKS' MATHEMATICS AND ASTRONOMY DIFFER FROM THE BABYLONIANS'?

The fifth and the fourth centuries BCE Greeks believed that the Earth was at the center of a finite universe and that the Earth was circled by the moon, Sun, and five visible planets, Mercury, Venus, Mars, Jupiter, and Saturn. Aristotle (384–322 BCE) describes this system of concentric spheres in his *On the Heavens*. His view of the universe was influential into the Middle Ages and in the Roman Catholic Church and the universities that were founded after the eleventh century, down to the seventeenth century.

Early Greek astronomers, such as Eudoxus of Cnidus (d. 355 BCE) used a system of concentric planetary rings or spheres and uniform circular motion of the planets quite exactly. In the second century CE, Ptolemy of Alexandria used the plane and solid geometry of Euclid, but without using numeric mathematics as the Late Babylonians had. His astronomical system was much more complicated than Eudoxus's and Aristotle's[20].

---

20. Gosselin 1985 Notes.

EXCURSUS 2

We can assume there were earlier Greek geometers than Euclid. However, when Euclid wrote his Thirteen Books of the Elements, *he mentioned none of his predecessors and his own work was so thorough that those who did precede him were easily forgotten. Three and a half centuries later, Ptolemy used Euclid's* Elements *to construct his planetary models which had moving parts. Ptolemy also knew how to combine velocities. Such models are cinematical. Cinematics[21] is a branch of mathematics that deals with motion, but with no regard for masses and forces (with which Newtonian kinematics would later concern itself). In addition, Ptolemy was able to predict planetary positions very accurately, given this cinematical approach.[22]*

We are taught in high school and often in college, too, that Ptolemy's astronomical system was Earth centered (geocentric), and that the moon, Sun, and planets revolve about the Earth in perfect circular motion. This description of Ptolemy's astronomy is not accurate. It was Aristotle's view of the universe that was absolutely geocentric, similar to the earth-centered model of Eudoxus. The Scholastic philosophers and theologians of the later Middle Ages (after 1100 CE) and Renaissance (1350–1600 CE) actually based their ideas on Aristotle, and not on Ptolemy.

When Ptolemy wrote The Almagest, *his preface "paid respect" to Aristotle's universe and his principle of the uniform circular motion of the heavenly bodies.[23] But later in the* Almagest, *Ptolemy ignores Aristotle's ideas on perfectly circular planetary motion and, instead, introduces an equant point that is outside the Earth.[24] The* Almagest's *purpose is positional. Given the time and your location, in what direction do you have to look to see any particular planet?*

Ptolemy
Woodcut by T. Stimmer, 1587

---

21. Cinematics is preferred by historians of ancient science to kinematics, so I am using it here.

22. Aaboe 2001, 135.

23. Ibid., 100.

24. Gosselin 1985, Notes.

But was there more to Ptolemy's astronomy than this? The answer to this question did not come until the 1960s. Yale's historians of ancient science were certain that Ptolemy's other text, The Planetary Hypotheses *(i.e., "Models"), which they knew existed from the* Hypotosis of Astronomical Models *by the Neoplatonist philosopher Proclus (412–485 CE), should give Ptolemy's entire cosmological system. However, all known extant editions of Planetary Hypotheses had only Book One which did not give the models of how the planets moved.*

Quite by accident, Bernard R. Goldstein, then at Yale and now emeritus at the University of Pittsburgh, discovered a microfilm of a 1242 CE Arabic translation of the Planetary Hypotheses *that contained Book Two, and it was this book that gave Ptolemy's cosmological system of the equant point somewhat off of the Earth's position and nesting spheres.*[25]

Book Two shows that each planet circles the Earth's equant point at greater and lesser distances, each within its own sphere on a deferent around whose end point each planet's epicycle moves. Aaboe called this "schlepping and woggling," i.e., each planet moves forward and backward in its apparent motion as we see it from the Earth, as each proceeds in its annual revolution around the equant point (not around the Earth itself). This meant that the planets did

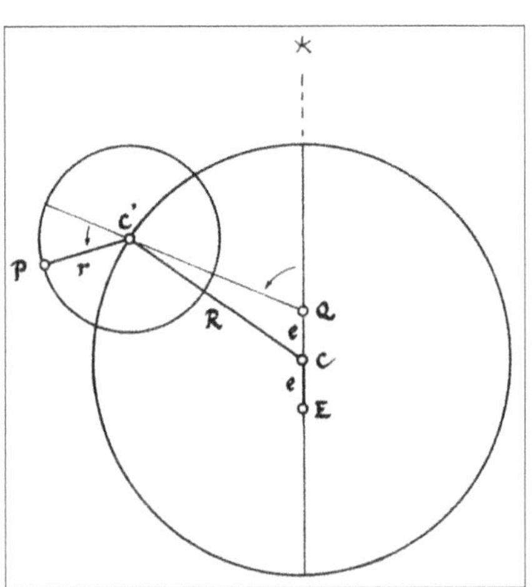

FIGURE 3: The Ptolemaic model of planetary motion around the Earth

not move around the Earth in perfect circles. As we will see, Ptolemy's planetary models' motions were very similar to planetary motions as they would be described by Johannes Kepler some fifteen hundred years later.

Book Two of Planetary Hypotheses *describes Ptolemy's nested spheres This means that the greatest distance of one planet from the Earth as that planet moves around its epicycle within its sphere, is the closest distance to the next planet's closest position to the Earth in its sphere. ("It is not conceivable that there is in nature a vacuum or any useless thing," wrote*

---

25. Aaboe 2001, 116-17, and Goldstein 1967.

Ptolemy, quoting Aristotle.) In this way, Ptolemy was able to show how far he determined each planet was from the Earth and, ultimately, the distance to the "fixed Stars" themselves (all computed in terrestrial radii.[26] Accordingly,

	d	*D*
Moon	*33*	*64*
Mercury	*64*	*166*
Venus	*166*	*1079**
Sun	*1160***	*1260*
Mars	*1260*	*8820*
Jupiter	*8820*	*14189*
Saturn	*14189*	*19865*
Fixed Stars	*19865*	

** and **: There is one aberration (Venus and Sun, above, my emphases). This was due to a complicated variance because Ptolemy used Hipparchus's fig-ures in this instance.[27] Ultimately, we see from the above table that Ptolemy says that the Fixed Stars are 19,865 terrestrial radii from us.[28] We see how small the "closed universe" of ancient and medieval times really was.[29]*

Aristotle's *Physics* described natural motion in the Earthly sphere, which included the Earth and the sky between the Earth and the Moon as being either horizontal or vertical. A stone, for example, which is thrown into the air will fall to the ground because its weight causes it

---

26. The radius of the Earth is measured from the center of the earth to the surface. It is about 3958 miles. The Ancient Greeks and Romans used "stades" but, when converted to miles, their measurements were quite close to modern measurements for the size of the Earth.

27. Aaboe 2001, 120-8, for a technical discussion of Ptolemy's nested spheres. Ptolemy's distances from the Earth to the Sun and other planets are nowhere near accurate. (Sophisticated telescopes are necessary to determine accurate distances to the planets.) The distance to the Moon is possibly more accurate than the other figures he gives. In essence, he was guessing.

28. This would mean that the fixed stars are only 78,466,750 miles from Earth. But we know today that the distance from Earth to the nearest star outside our solar system (Proxima Centauri) is 4.24 light years. Chapter 5 will revisit the issue of Proxima Centauri and its exoplanet, Proxima Centauri b in some detail.

29. See Koyré 1957.

to seek its natural or proper place, i.e., the Earth. Aristotle also taught that Earth is composed of four elements (Earth, water, fire, and air). He believed that Earth is at the center of the universe precisely because it is the heaviest of these elements. Motion in the skies, from the Moon to the extremity of the finite universe, is, on the other hand, perfect and therefore circular, according to Aristotle.[30]

The Greeks thought planets and stars were flawless because the human eye could see no evidence of their shapes being corrupted by mountains, valleys, or water, and they therefore assumed, with the exception of Ptolemy, that these celestial bodies were capable only of circular motion within a celestial perfection that existed beyond any need for further explanation. (Much of what was accepted as science came to be considered religious philosophy and would be embraced as the basis for religious truths by the late medieval, Renaissance, and seventeenth-century Aristotelians.)

The works of Classical Graeco-Roman culture were largely lost after the fall of the Western Roman Empire in the fifth-century CE. Whatever classical texts did survive were often stored in the librairies of the monastic orders after this time. Plato's books were lost, and the only one that was partially known was the *Timaeus*.[31] After the birth of the Muslim prophet Muhammad (570–632 CE) and the consequent spread of Islam throughout the Middle East, North Africa, and into Spain, Arabic scholars adopted Graeco-Roman works in mathematics, astronomy, medicine, astrology, alchemy, and philosophy. Al-Kindi (805–870 CE), Al-Haitbam (ca. 965–1039 CE) in Cairo, Al-Battani and Thabit bin Qurra (both fl. ninth century) began the Islamic studies of the Ptolemaic system. Other Islamic scholars continued this work into the eleventh and twelfth centuries.[32] Their studies translated and

---

30. Pedersen 2009, 105-110.

31. P. O. Kristeller 1961, passim. Platonism and Middle Platonism continued to be known in the Eastern Roman Empire (Byzantine Empire). The Florentine philosopher, Marsilio Ficino, translated all of Plato's dialogues, based on access to monastic and Byzantine collections, by 1484; the first printed edition of Plato's works in the original Greek was published in Venice in 1513 by Aldus Manutius. In this way, Plato's philosophy became known in Western Europe in its entirety for the first time since Antiquity. Ficino also edited the works of Proclus and Plotinus, the late Ancient Middle Platonist and Neoplatonist.

32. See Pedersen 2009, 153-165, for a discussion of the contributions of the scholars in the Islamic Mediterranean world.

studied basically only Aristotle, Ptolemy, and their late Ancient commentators. They displayed little or no interest in Graeco-Roman literary, poetic, or historical works.

When the Arabs conquered the Hispanic peninsula in the seventh and eighth centuries CE, Jewish scholars there also began to translate Aristotle's scientific works, as well as those of Avicenna and Averroës, and other Arabic scholars, into Hebrew and thence into Latin. By the eleventh and twelfth centuries universities were created in Paris, Oxford, Bologna, Padua, Palermo, and elsewhere. As this happened, Aristotle's and Ptolemy's works, the only known philosophical and scientific texts from Antiquity, became available for the first time in Christian Western Europe, along with their Arabic commentators' works. It was in this way that the astronomical systems of Aristotle and Ptolemy were introduced to these new European universities. These were the only sciences that were taught until the sixteenth century.

In 1277, Étienne Tempier and the Faculty of Theology at the University of Paris found that 277 propositions of Aristotle were contrary to Christian doctrine (teachings such as the eternity of the world) and these "errors" were removed from the manuscripts of Aristotle's texts as the professors taught them to their students. Once the Aristotelian corpus had been Christianized, Aristotle's and his commentators' works were used as scientific textbooks in all the European universities

One major work that developed from the knowledge of Aristotle and Ptolemy in the later Middle Ages was *On the Sphere* (*De sfera*) by Johannes de Sacrobosco (John of Holywood, c. 1195–1256 CE) which was a somewhat simplified compilation of these works. It was required university reading until the seventeenth century.[33]

Medieval mathematicians and students of nature found even Euclid so difficult that these students could no get beyond the Fifth Proposition of Euclid's First Book of *The Elements of Geometry*;

> *"In isosceles triangles the angles at the base are equal to one another....If the equal straight lines be* [sic] *produced further, the angles under the base will be equal to one another."*

---

33. See Oosterhoff 2015 for a discussion of how Sacrobosco's *Sphere* was read and how its content was understood.

For that reason, the Fifth Proposition was called the "pons asino-rum" (the "bridge of fools"), meaning those lacking sufficient education or understanding could go no further than the 5th proposition of the total of 465 in the thirteen books of Euclid's *Elements*.

(In addition, Christianized Aristotelianism was absorbed into late medieval literature. Dante Alighieri (1265–1321 CE) filled his *Inferno*, the first book of his *Divina Commedia,* with Ptolemaic-Aristotelian astronomical ideas: e.g., the Earth is at the center of the finite universe, and Hell is at the center of the Earth; Satan himself is at Hell's and the Earth's frozen center, because he is to be found, following incrementally immoral and subterranean steps, at the absolute central spot of the universe, the one furthest from God and his Love. It is paradoxical that in this medieval view, man, whom Christ had come to save, lives on the surface of this central Earth which is also so close to the eternal abode of Lucifer, God's greatest enemy.)[34]

Arab and Christian astronomical observers found problems with the original Ptolemaic view of the universe. To understand what happened, we must return to some of the details about the Ptolemaic System. Ptolemy believed in a finite universe, but, as we saw, one with nested spheres for each of the five known planets, the moon, and Sun. While the Babylonians' universe was based on arithmetic computations, the early Greek astronomers had not been able to achieve such accuracy precisely because the planets do not move in perfect circles. Accordingly, Ptolemy and other Greek astronomers of the later Hellenistic period tried to explain the apparent (though false) fact that planets seemed to stop, move backward, and then forward again, using eccentric epicycles to show the backward and forward motions they thought occurred, and to get observations and explanations to work accurately together. (See **Figure 3**.) And, as observations became more accurate with the development of the astrolabe, later medieval Arabic astronomers, using the Greek system, had to add epicycles built upon epicycles to explain planetary motion. In modern parlance, this created an "explanatory crisis" that eventually collapsed

---

34. Dante followed Aristotle by having the Earth at the center of the universe, not Ptolemy's equant point of the Earth. However, Dante did continue Ptolemy's nested spheres. See Dante 1970: *Paradiso*, Canto 2, line 29: "To God, who has raised us now to the first star [the Moon]...." This is Ptolemy's first sphere.

the way astronomical motions were explained and called for a new explanation, i.e., a new paradigm.[35]

In the summer of 1572, a "star" appeared in the heavens. (We now realize it was a supernova.) In 1579 a comet cut across the skies. Tycho Brahe (1546–1601 CE) showed that these two objects were beyond the moon and could not be attributable to meteors. They were therefore not foreseeable according to Aristotelian or Ptolemaic astronomical beliefs about the perfection of the heavens. The old "normal" science that had lasted since 350 BCE and 150 CE could not explain these events. A new paradigm was needed to replace it.[36]

NICHOLAS COPERNICUS'S DE REVOLUTIONIBUS TO THE TIME OF GALILEO

The seismic shift in scientific outlook (which many think was the only Scientific Revolution) had its beginning in the sixteenth century with the work of the Polish priest, Nicholas Copernicus, (1473–1543 CE).

Copernicus was born in Toruń, Poland, and went to the University of Cracow. Copernicus began to collect crude instruments with which he could observe the heavens. He then went to the University of Bologna in Italy where he began to study for a degree in Canon Law.[37] He later completed his studies and received a doctorate in Canon Law at Ferrara.

---

35. In 1962 Thomas Kuhn challenged the view that "normal" science progresses with the simple accumulation of data. Rather, he argued, "normal" science eventually fails to answer questions or solve problems and a revolution occurs which creates a new governing paradigmatic theory, a new science, as in the way Einstein's Relativity would supplant the Newtonian view of the world. In this case, Newton's laws are still valid until objects approach "c," the speed of light. The same is true for the quantum mechanical revolution of Niels Bohr (1885–1962): Galileo's mechanics are still valid, but Bohr's quantum mechanical laws are needed to explain the sub-atomic world.

Although Bohr proposed new laws (e.g., the instantaneous transition of electrons from one orbit to another within the atom), his theories came to be called the "old quantum mechanics." It was supplanted in the mid 1920s by the new quantum mechanics of Werner Heisenberg, Erwin Schrödinger, and others. Bohr's quantum mechanics is now seen as a primitive step in the direction of the real explanations of the new quantum mechanics.

One can see, then, that science proceeds in revolutionary steps. It always has from the Babylonians to Ptolemy, to Copernicus, to Galileo and Newton, to Einstein and Bohr, Heisenberg, Schrödinger, and beyond.

36. Ferguson 2001, 55-6.

37. Church Law.

He followed this with a brief visit home after which he returned to Italy and went to the University of Padua. There, he met astronomers and mathematicians, but turned to medicine which he practiced as a canon (a minor priest) when he eventually returned to Toruń.

While in Italy Copernicus had also learned Greek, which made him a literary scholar familiar with the ancient Classical literature that was so popular and influential in the Renaissance period. Working in obscurity, he published a small book in 1512, titled *Commentariolus*. In this book, Copernicus placed the Sun at the center of the universe, and put the earth in motion around the Sun. This of course ran counter to what astronomers thought they could conclude from their naked-eye observations of the heavens and by using "normal" Aristotelian and Ptolemaic science as an *explanation*, as well as counter to what most ancient and medieval authors had written. For example, believers in the unmoving Earth had said that if it moved, all things would have to be anchored on it lest everything blow off the Earth as it moved: swords, hats, birds, humans, and so forth.

Nevertheless, there had been two ancient Greek authors who had written counter to the general ideas about the heavenly bodies. Philolaos of Croton (470–c.385 BCE) and Aristarchus of Samos (310–c. 230 BCE) believed that the Sun was the center of the universe (making the geo-centric system into a heliocentric one), with all the then known planets and the Earth circling the Sun. Copernicus was influenced by these two recently discovered Greek texts. Other important influences included contemporary Italian philosophers, especially the Florentine Neoplatonist Marsilio Ficino (1433–1499 CE). Ficino's important book, *De sole* (*On the Sun*), argued that the Sun is God's Light in the universe and that the power of this light (*Lux*) causes all motion in the world. It has been argued[38] that Ficino's book on the Sun introduced the Solar Age of the sixteenth and seventeenth centuries wherein the Sun became important as the center of the universe and as a purveyor of God's Will and influence.

Ficino himself had been influenced by a supposed very ancient thinker named Hermes Trismegistus (Hermes the Thrice Great) whose writings, *The Hermetica*, were thought to predate Moses and suppos-edly had even influenced the Egyptian Sun-centered monotheism of

---

38. Garin 1958.

the Pharaoh Akhenaten (died c. 1334 BCE). The Hermetic books were very mystical and religious. It is not surprising, then, that Copernicus's *De revolutionibus* (*On the Revolutions of the Heavenly Bodies*, as it is popularly known in English) contained a reference, just after his diagram of the heliocentric universe, to Hermes Trismegistus as well as to other ancient literary works, indicating that the solar universe carried with it an ancient religious framework.

> *"In the center of all this resides the Sun. Who indeed in this most magnificent...temple would put light in another, or in a better place than the One wherefrom it...could at the same time illuminate the whole of it. Therefore it is not improper that...some people call it the lamp of the world, others its mind, others its ruler. Trismegistus [calls the Sun] the visible God, Sophocles' Electra [calls it] the All-Seeing. Thus, assuredly, as residing in the royal see, the Sun governs the surrounding family of the Stars."*

In one of the Hermetic books (*Asclepius*), Hermes Trismegistus says that the Sun illuminates the planets not just by the power of its light but also by its "divinity and holiness," and adds that the Sun is the "second God." Clearly, Copernicus, mathematician, astronomer, and priest, had ancient as well as Renaissance literature in mind in both his 1512 *Commentariolus* and his 1543 *De revolutionibus*, the works that introduce the new "solar age of the universe," at the beginning of the so-called Scientific Revolution.[39]

In 1543, as he lay on his deathbed in Toruń, Copernicus received the first published edition of his *De revolutionibus*. Delirious with fever, Copernicus was unable to read the unsigned preface to his book, which was placed just before his own dedicatory epistle to Pope Paul III at the beginning of the book. This anonymous preface claimed, as if it were in Copernicus's own words, that this work on the sun-centered universe was not "true." (It was not known until the late sixteenth century that it was

---

39. The Calvinist scholar Isaac Casaubon discovered in 1614 that Hermes Trismegistus never existed and that the Hermetic texts attributed to him were actually written in the second century CE in Alexandria, Egypt. Early Christian, Jewish, Platonic, Neoplatonic, and Zoroastrian ideas and cults all coexisted in Alexandria in the second century, so it is no wonder that the *Hermetica* had such a ring of ancient truth. Even after 1614, intellectuals continued to believe in the veracity of the doctrines found in the Corpus Hermeticism because of the familiar collection of ideas found in them.

not Copernicus who had asserted the hypothetical nature of his book, and that the unsigned and misleading preface had actually been written by a disciple of Martin Luther, Andreas Osiander (1498–1552 CE). Despite this forged disclaimer, however, Copernicus's description of what he believed to be a religiously based heliocentric universe in *De revolutionibus* slowly began to garner considerable attention by the late sixteenth century.[40]

Copernicus's goal was to rescue the skies from the complexity of his late medieval Catholic and Arabic Aristotelian-Ptolemaic predecessors, but he never really achieved this simplification. Among other things, his system actually complicated his Ptolemaic and his Arabic predecessors' planetary systems because he added secondary epicycles.[41] As a result, Copernicus did not immediately inspire other astronomers to abandon their Aristotelian-Ptolemaic views. Still, the discussion of Copernicus finally became quite fashionable in the royal courts of late sixteenth-century Europe. Poets such as Pierre de Ronsard (1524–1585 CE) and Pontus de Tyard (1521–1605 CE) at the French courts of Charles IX, Henri III, and Henri IV (1560–1610), Thomas Digges of the Elizabethan court, and the Englishman John Dee at the Emperor Rudolph II's court in Prague, were all sympathetic in one degree or another to the Copernican theory.[42] At the very least they found it the basis of entertaining discourse in their patrons' courts. Such discourse, after all, was the goal of court life.

These debates influenced the Italian anti-Aristotelian philosopher Giordano Bruno (1548–1600) who had visited these courts in hope of finding patronage. Bruno expounded his views on a mystical version of Copernicanism in his *Cena de le Ceneri*[43] and in four other Italian dialogues that he wrote and published in London in 1584 and 1585. As we have seen in Chapter 3, he was condemned and burned as a heretic in Rome on February 17, 1600. The Roman Catholic Inquisition did not condemn Bruno just for his apostasy from the Dominican Order, but probably even more so for his arguments on the mobility of the Earth and the infinity of the universe.[44]

Nevertheless, Bruno was later hailed by anti-Papists in late nineteenth-century Italy as a pioneering Copernican and a martyr for

---

40. Gingrich 2004; Westman 2011.
41. Neugebauer 1983, 132, 318; Copernicus thus added epicycles upon epicycles.
42. Yates 1947/1989, passim.
43. Bruno 1584; Gosselin and Lerner 1986.
44. Marinez 2016.

science. This showed a misunderstanding of Bruno, for he was certainly not a scientist in the way Copernicus and Galileo were.[45]

Johannes Kepler (1571–1630), a con-temporary of Galileo, utilized a form of Copernicanism in his *Mysterium cosmographicum* (1596), just before he also arrived at the court of Rudolph II in Prague where matters concern-ing alchemy and *mathesis* (mysti-cal mathematics) were given a great deal of attention. In his book, Kepler espoused a heliocentrism that deviated from that of Copernicus and Galileo via an extreme mysticism which can be described as a neo-Pythagorean numerical system infused with reli-gion. Kepler's astronomer-employer,

Kepler in 1620
Artist unknown

Tycho Brahe (1546–1601), also did not solely embrace Copernicanism. Rather he had proposed a geo-heliocentric cosmology based on both the Ptolemaic and Copernican systems. Brahe, who was recognized as the most accurate naked-eye astronomer of his time, believed that the Sun and the Earth's moon circle the central and unmoving Earth, while the other planets within this closed world orbit the Sun. in this way, Tycho Brahe hybridized the traditional, Church-accepted Aristotelian view of the universe with the new Copernican view.

Nonetheless, the Roman Catholic Church held fast to the traditional Aristotelian-Ptolemaic cosmology until 1837, even though several astronomers and scientists had completely discredited this view by the early eighteenth century. One could add the strange fact that Jesuits in China had tried to teach Copernicanism to the Chinese in the late sixteenth and early seventeenth centuries. However, because of the Church's hostility to the Copernican theory after 1616 (see below), the Jesuits were unable to offer either clear or accurate explanations of it to the Chinese scholars who had in fact seemed to be willing to learn about heliocentrism.[46]

---

45. Lerner and Gosselin 1973.
46. Sivin 1973.

THE EARLY YEARS OF GALILEO

Among early-modern dissident scientists, Galileo was the most well known to the Roman Catholic Church and, after Bruno's execution in 1600, he was considered the most threatening to the Church and its belief systems.

Galileo Galilei was born in Pisa, Italy, on February 15, 1564, three days before the death of Michelangelo Buonarotti and two months prior to the birth of William Shakespeare. Galileo was the oldest of seven children, and his father, Vincenzo Galilei, was a noted lutenist and musical theorist. After some early schooling in Florence, Galileo entered a nearby monastery with the intention of joining its monastic order. He very much enjoyed the quiet, studious life of the monastery. However, his

Galileo Galilei in 1624
by Ottavio Leoni (detail)

father altered his vocational path, returned Galileo to Florence in order to complete his early studies and prepare him to go to the University of Pisa as a student of medicine. While at the university, Galileo began to find fault with its Aristotelian teachings, and he started private studies with a teacher of mathematics. He also began his own study of Euclid's *Thirteen Books of the Elements*. As his interest in mathematics progressed, he lost interest in pursuing a medical degree and he eventually left the university without completing his studies in that field. He continued his private studies and found himself increasingly overwhelmed by a love of mathematics.

By the time he was twenty-two, Galileo had written his first scientific treatise and had been teaching mathematics in Florence and Siena, His mathematical abilities had become well known and, as a result, he was asked to give a lecture to the prestigious Florentine Academy on the size, location, and arrangement of Hell as depicted in Dante's *Inferno*.

Galileo was given a chair in mathematics in 1589 at the University of Pisa, and he began to practice physical experiments. Years before, when he had been a student at Pisa, Galileo had already noticed inconsistencies in the *Physics* of Aristotle. In particular, he began studying motion and its relation to weight. He dropped objects of different weights, but of the same material and noticed that they seemed to reach the ground at the same time. This result ran counter to Aristotle's law of motion which asserted that objects of different weights, should reach the ground at different times. Galileo does note that his objects reached the ground "at almost the same time." He further said, "I hope you will make nothing of the fact that there was this slight difference in arrival at the ground." This last statement was symptomatic of Galileo's ability to see beyond Aristotelian teaching, and understand that his experiments (or "experiences," as he called them) might have the slightest differences in outcome due to the minimal failures in his ability to construct the perfect "tests in nature," or "experiences." It was this clear-sighted rational thinking that allowed Galileo to proceed as a scientist in the years that followed.

Galileo moved to Venice where he used what he called a "spyglass"[47] to convince the Doge and the Venetian Senate that he ought to be hired to teach at the distinguished University of Padua.[48] He perfected his telescope's refraction so that it could see farther, and, he argued, it could be used on the shoreline of Venice as well as on Venetian ships to spot enemy ships before the human eye alone could seem them. He made a famous demonstration to the Doge and other officials from the top of the bell tower (Campanile) at the cathedral of San Marco to show how far one could see with his "spyglass."

Duly impressed, in 1609 Doge Leonardo Donato gave Galileo an appointment at the University of Padua with tenure for life. Soon Galileo began to negotiate for a preferable position with the Grand Duke Cosimo II de' Medici of Florence-Tuscany. As a client of the Duke, he hoped to be given the prestigious position of mathematician and philosopher in the Florentine court, which was quite an

---

47. Galileo had developed his telescope in 1597, although it had first been developed in Holland by Hans Lipperhey.

48. Padua was in the area ruled by Venice (the Veneto) and so the Venetian state could make appointments to the university there.

improvement over being a university professor. Once again Galileo brought his "spyglass" to persuade Grand Duke Cosimo II of his ability to add lustre and exciting conversation to the Florentine ducal court. Whereas he had presented his "spyglass" as he approached the Venetian Doge, he now referred to it as a telescope, a scientific instrument for seeing planets and stars more clearly. The Grand Duke was impressed, and in 1610 he became the new patron of Galileo who would henceforth be known as mathematician and philosopher of the Florentine ducal court. In fact, Galileo appears to have been among the highest paid of all the courtiers who were in the pay of the Grand Duke of Florence-Tuscany.[49]

His first important presentation to the Grand Duke was a book Galileo had written in Padua and had published in 1610, entitled *The Starry Messenger* (*Sidereus nuncius*). On the title page he called himself "Professor of Mathematics in the University of Padua and Gentleman of Florence." He announced that he had discovered four new stars (moons) surrounding Jupiter, whch he called the Medicean Stars in honor of Grand Duke Cosimo II whose horoscope planet was Jupiter. Cosimo II's name was thus attached to these "stars" in the skies "from the beginning of time to the end of time," a kind of gift that no one had ever before been able to give to his sponsor. As Galileo added, "Four stars were reserved for your illustrious name."[50] Galileo had observed these so-called stars with his telescope which he had perfected so much that the Earth's moon, Jupiter, and its moons all seemed "one thousand times larger and thirty times closer than they did by natural [naked-eye] vision."[51]

Discussing his telescopic view of Earth's moon in *The Starry Messenger*, he described "large and small spots," and concluded that the moon's surface was not smooth or perfectly spherical, as Aristotle had said, but "full of mountains and valleys similar to those on the Earth."[52]

---

49. Biagioli 1993, 104: "As far as I can tell, Galileo's salary was among the ten highest of the grand duchy of Tuscany at that time." Cf. also n. 4 on that page.

50. Ibid., 129.

51. Galileo's telescope is today on view in the Museo Galileo, Piazza dei Giudici, 1, in Florence. It is remarkable how simple his telescope was. It appears much like the type of telescope parents might buy for their children.

52. Galileo made trigonometric calculations using the shadows of the mountains, from which he could estimate their heights and realized they were comparable to the heights of terrestrial mountains.

Accordingly, Galileo reasoned that the moon as well as Jupiter and its satellites are also terrestrial, i.e., like the Earth, and were distinct from the Sun and other stars. This was an important argument against the Aristotelian and Ptolemaic beliefs that all heavenly bodies were perfect and completely unlike Earth.

This was enough, in addition to Galileo's previous writings, to earn him many enemies in the Church's religious orders, especially the Dominicans and the Jesuits which were the Church's most prominent teaching monastic orders.[53] Finally, as if the Church needed any further reason to be alarmed, Galileo's *Starry Messenger* signified his official advocacy of the Copernican Theory, the heliocentric system whose ancillary teaching of the universe's infinity and infinite number of worlds and lives, proposed by Giordano Bruno in 1584-5, had been the basis for the charge of "obstinate heresy" against Bruno and the reason why he was burned at the stake in 1600.

GALILEO TEACHES THE THEOLOGIANS

In 1616, Galileo was called to Rome to meet with Cardinal Robert Bellarmine. Bellarmine was a very learned Jesuit scholar and was opposed to the Copernican Theory.[54] Bellarmine told Galileo that he could not teach the Copernican Theory because it was "false and opposed to Holy Scripture."

The previous year Galileo had written a manuscript in Italian on the issue of Science versus the Bible. it was titled *Letter to the Grand Duchess Christina* (of Tuscany). In this text, Galileo argues that there are two truths: the truth of the Bible and the

Robert Cardinal Bellarmine
Unknown artist

truth of Nature (Science). Neither of these truths can be wrong; they must be in accord. When Nature and Science seem to be in contradiction

53. Santillana 1955.

54. Bellarmine had served on the Roman Inquisition that had condemned Bruno.

to the Bible, it is the duty of "wise expositors" of the Bible to interpret the Bible's words so that they agree with the truths of Science and Nature. In other words, Galileo argues that the understanding of the Bible must bend to the truths of Science. Indeed, Science is based on facts, and there can only be one interpretation of scientific facts.

Galileo clearly states in the *Letter to the Grand Duchess* that he is a follower of Copernicus. Admitting that the Bible has passages that indicate that the Sun and planets go around the geocentric Earth (e.g., Joshua 10:12-13 [KJV]), he says. "Whenever the Bible speaks about any physical conclusion,..." the rule has been observed of avoiding confusion in the minds of the common people "that would make them doubt the ethical and religious teachings of the Bible." Hence, Galileo argues, theologians should accept the teachings of Science while realizing that the Bible did not have these truths in mind when it was written for less educated readers. If the theologians followed this advice, there would be no conflict between Religion and Science.

The manuscript of the *Letter to the Grand Duchess* was not widely read when it was penned in 1615. Few contemporaries knew that Galileo had thrown down the gauntlet with the Church in his self-appointed role as a Copernican advisor to the theologians. (The *Letter* was not published until 1636.) And so when Galileo published his *Dialogue on the Two Chief World Systems, Ptolemaic and Copernican* in 1632, the Master of the Holy Palace, Niccoló Riccardo, having been told about the 1615 *Letter*, asked for a copy of the manuscript. One can easily imagine what Galileo's Dominican and Jesuit enemies thought of the *Letter to the Grand Duchess* when they finally got a chance to read it.

VATICAN PATRONAGE IN THE SEVENTEENTH CENTURY AND HOW IT WORKED FOR AND AGAINST GALILEO

Scholars, poets, and artists of the sixteenth and seventeenth centuries relied on rich patrons to support their work and lives. As we have seen, the Venetian court's support of Galileo gained him a university professorship as well as the kind of distinction that helped gain him entrée to the Grand Duke of Florence and the patronage of that Medici prince.

During his visit to Rome in 1616, Galileo had hoped for patronage from officials of the Roman Catholic Church, but instead found himself in some difficulties with the Church because he had come to be seen as a proponent of Copernicus's teaching. Instead of receiving patronage, he was sternly warned by Cardinal Bellarmine never again to advocate the truth of Copernican heliocentrism in his teaching or writing.

Philosophers and theologians were often able to secure jobs in universities that provided courses to teach and colleges in which to live, but anti-Aristotelian philosophers found that they could only travel from court to court throughout Europe in search of a prince who would not only tolerate their views but would be willing to finance their livelihoods on a grander scale than universities could afford. (Giordano Bruno is an example of a wandering scholar whose personality prevented him from from finding a permanent sponsor.) The field of patronage seekers was crowded and intense, and rewarded only those whose works and ideas could provide exciting discussions in courts. The kings and queens of England, the kings of Spain and France, and the Holy Roman Emperor all injected prestige into their courts because they were patrons of the arts and sciences. Galileo's own patrons can be counted among the dukes of smaller regions who wished to instill the same sort of prestige into their courts of Venice and Florence and, after 1623, Galileo sought the patronage of the highest religious court (Rome), and so he sought the patronage of Matteo Barberini when he became Pope Urban VIII.

Once a patron was found, a scholar like Galileo could still not be assured of any security after his patron died or, for that matter, even while he lived. This was especially true within the papal regimes, but Galileo had reason to believe that he had obtained the long-term patronage of Pope Urban VIII.

The Tribulations and Eventual Triumph of Matteo Barberini

Matteo Barberini (1568–1644) was a person who himself had continuously sought higher positions or favor in the papal court, long before he became pope. Well born to begin with, he was made papal ambassador to the French court by Pope Clement VIII, but after Clement's death on March 5, 1605, the learned Barberini had to leave the papal court until the new pope, Leo XI, elected pope on April 1, died less than a month later, on April 27, 1605. Patronage for Matteo began again with the next pope, Paul V, amid the wreckage of the careers of those who had just begun to enjoy the support of the suddenly dead Pope Leo. Paul V reigned until 1621. Soon after the beginning of his reign, Pope Paul made Matteo Barberini a cardinal-priest (1606). Now considered a prince of the Church and having inherited a vast sum of his money from his uncle, Cardinal Barberini built a magnificent palace in Rome and began his own patronage system. During the two years after the death of Pope Paul V, Gregory XV was pope, and upon his death in 1623, Matteo Barberini became Pope Urban VIII. He had completed his difficult climb through the tumultuous world of papal patronage to the height of Christendom. His career was a good example of how precarious one's position at the papal court could oftentimes be, even though he was well born and a cleric.

BACK TO GALILEO

When Pope Clement VIII had died, "Barberini wept and sighed most bitterly...because of the tragedy of the pope's death, but even more so for seeing his career wrecked." Galileo's position as a courtier in Florence and a would-be courtier in Rome was just as precarious, if not more so. As we shall see, he fell out of favor with Urban VIII and, when that happened, he, previously the favorite in the Florentine ducal court, fell out of favor there, too. The Baroque court, whether in Rome or Florence, was always unstable.[55]

Intellectuals were delighted at the elevation of Barberini to the papacy, as they thought his learned background made it likely he would enjoy readings and discussions in his court. Numbering himself among this group of hopeful patronage seekers, Galileo at first did become a favorite of Pope Urban. Yet he had not paid careful attention to the vagaries of papal court life, as could be seen even from the career of Matteo Barberini himself. Galileo's favor and security in papal Rome proved to be illusory, and it is difficult to ascertain whether he was ever as strongly entrenched as a papal courtier as he believed.[56] When he fell, he fell quickly and hard, as we shall see.

55. Biagioli 1993, 319-23.
56. Op. cit.

The Dialogue on the Two Great World Systems

Pope Urban VIII urged Galileo to write a book on the Copernican vision of the universe and to compare it to the Ptolemaic system. Galileo thought that this charge countered Cardinal Robert Bellarmine's 1616 order not to teach or to write on the Copernican system. Yet there was a warning in Pope Urban's words to Galileo. He was to show, the Pope said, how the Ptolemaic system was correct and Copernicanism wrong. Indeed, the Pope's admonition on this matter was to be clearly stated in the book he asked Galileo to write.

There are two important points to be made here. Clearly, Urban VIII intended that this book would be the sort that would allow for interesting discussion in the papal court, especially since the Pope required that his own summation was to be included in the book's conclusion. It was to be a work that a courtier was expected to write: not necessarily a profound work ferreting out new truth, but just interesting, and amenable to pleasant debate within the papal Curia, and one that would make Urban the arbiter in this discussion. In this regard, I think it was to be like the debates I mentioned having taken place in the French court in the 1580s between Pontus de Tyard and Pierre de Ronsard.[57]

Galileo finished *Il dialogo sopra i due massimi systemi del mondo* in March 1632. In order to have the book published within the contours of religious law, Galileo received a *nihil abstat* (an attestation by a Church official that "there is nothing objectionable"on doctrinal or moral grounds in the book), and an *imprimatur* ("it may be published") from Church officials in both Florence and Rome. The book was actually published in Florence.

The Dialogue on the Two Great World Systems was divided into four parts or "days" of conversations among three men: Salviati (Galileo's spokesman, giving the Copernican view), Simplicio (giving the Ptolemaic view), and Sagredo (the open-minded layman [who in real life was the banker from whom Galileo received his pay as a Florentine courtier]). Sagredo acted in this book as a kind of judge between the proponents of the two systems, and he gradually accepted Salviati's arguments and belittled Simplicio's.

---

57. See above, p. 99.

What I find particularly interesting in the *Dialogue* is the fact that, as Galileo presents the Copernican system, he does not make use of Johannes Kepler's argument in *De astronomia nova* (1609) that the planets circle the Sun in slightly elliptical orbits. Rather, like Copernicus and Aristotle long before him, Galileo described perfectly circular planetary paths. One explanation for Galileo's choosing to ignore Kepler's elliptical orbits may be that Galileo was a man of **High Renaissance** artistic values who eschewed **Mannerism's** love of artificiality and embellishment. This can be explained by examining, almost parenthetically at this point, the thesis of the art historian Erwin Panofsky, comparing these two artistic styles.

THE PANOFSKY THESIS EXPLAINS WHY GALIEO DID NOT ACCEPT KEPLER'S ELLIPTICAL ORBITS?

The art and cultural historian, Erwin Panofsky (1892–1968), suggested that Galileo's aesthetic judgments drove his scientific preferences.[58] Classical purism in music, art, and literature were of a kind with Galileo's classicism in science. Hence, Galileo preferred plain instrumental music and poetic style rather than late sixteenth-century Mannerist music and poetry where declamation included sobs and similar outbursts of emotion. His preferred poet was Ludovico Ariosto (1474–1533), author of *Orlando Furioso* (1516), not Torquato Tasso (1544–1593), author of *Gerusalemme liberata* (1580). The former provides a straight-forward narrative while the latter, in the Mannerist style, is full of outbursts of emotion and is complicated in its poetic style.

In art, Galileo followed a similar path. He liked the classical High Renaissance styles of Raphael and the early Michelangelo, while the stylistically complicated later Michelangelo as well as other artists such as Giorgio Vasari (1511–1574) and Tintoretto, known as *"il Furioso"* (1518–1594), followed Mannerist habits of adding figures in their paintings which made the "stories" shown by their paintings less clear, yet more emotional. Mannerist architects even added elliptical designs to the rectangular style which had been dominant in the earlier sixteenth-century classical High Renaissance.

---

58. Panofsky 1956, 3-15.

Galileo's simplicity of science resembled his simplicity of artistic and literary preferences, as is shown by his adoption of the classical, circular orbits of the Copernican system, rather than his venturing into the "Art and Wonder Room" (*Kunst-und-Wunderkammern*) of Mannerist Keplerian planetary motions. At a time when it was possible for there to be a close relationship between his cultural aesthetics and his new science, Galileo's art and literary judgments determined how he expressed what he observed in Nature and they simply did not allow him to reconcile his astronomical science with the Mannerist Johannes Kepler's elliptical planetary orbits around the Sun. Accordingly, the aesthetics of these two great contemporaneous scientists led each to two distinct understandings of how the planets moved.[59]

Some have argued that even though Galileo had received copies of Kepler's books with their elliptical-orbital arguments, he had simply not bothered to read them. It is true that Kepler wrote Galileo congratulating him on his work on Jupiter's moons. But it took Galileo seventeen years to respond to him. Kepler had mentioned others, such as Tycho Brahe, whose work combining both the Copernican and Ptolemaic systems might have been of use to Galileo, but the latter did not have good relations with the wider scientific community. Indeed, Kepler's teacher, Michael Mäistlin congratulated Kepler for having "plucked out Galileo's feathers."[60] So it is a question of either accepting Panofsky's argument about two different aesthetic styles or we are left with Galileo's reluctance to bother reading the views of Kepler, a rival scientist. Take your choice.

THE TRIAL AND CONDEMNATION OF GALILEO: THE EARTH IS ONCE AGAIN THE CENTER OF THE UNIVERSE

Galileo incurred the wrath of Pope Urban VIII and the Roman Inquisition for several reasons, not the least being his writings prior to *Il dialogo*. Pietro Redondi reports that he found a denunciation of Galileo's *Il saggiatore* (*The Assayer*, 1623) dating from 1624 in the Inquisition Archives that implied that his scientific theories were based on the ancient and medieval idea of Atomism that comes from the

59. Op. Cit.
60. Ferguson 2002, 323-6.

Hellenistic Greek philosopher Epicurus (342–270 BCE). His philosophy was transmitted to later ages in part through the Roman poet Lucretius (c. 99–c. 55 BCE) and his Epicurean epic poem, *De rerun natura (On the Nature of Things)*. Atomism is the belief that all things in nature are made up of tiny particles of matter. This materialist philosophy can be assumed to exclude anything spiritual. After the twelfth century, atomism ran counter to the Roman Catholic Church's doctrine of Transubstantiation, i.e., the doctrine that the consecrated bread and wine are transformed by the priest into the actual or real body and blood of Jesus during the "miracle" of the Mass. In an atomist's world, bread and wine can only be bread and wine. No transformation or transubstantiation of substances can take place.[61]

Galileo's *Il saggiatore* could also be linked to the fourteenth-century Master of Arts, Nicholas of Autrecourt (c. 1299–1369 CE). His atomistic, anti-Eucharist ideas were condemned by the Faculty of Theology at the University of Paris.

On November 25, 1347, Nicolas's manuscripts, at least as many as could be found for the occasion, were burned in front of the university and he was divested of his degree of Master of Arts and his ability to teach in the university. He was never again active as a scholar or professor. He left Paris and moved to Metz in the Lorraine area of France. Metz was an imperial city governed by Louis the Bavarian and safely away from Paris and its strictures against him. There, Nicholas received the benefit of canon and became dean of the chapter at the cathedral of Metz in 1350. Nothing more was heard of him until his death nineteen years later.[62]

It was only quite by chance that one of his manuscripts that had escaped burning that November day was found in the early twentieth century and his philosophy suddenly became known again. Something like this could have happened to Galileo, had his books been burned, assigning him also to oblivion.

The fear that Galileo might have been an Epicurean atomist did earn him the enmity of the Jesuits in 1624, and they were eager to bring new charges against him when his *Dialogue on the Two Great World Systems* was published eight years later.

---

61. Redondi 1987.
62. Autrecourt 1971.

For all intents and purposes, Galileo's 1632-1633 trial before the Roman Inquisition was centered on the *Dialogue on the Two Great World Systems* itself, because it had angered Pope Urban. Galileo had agreed to put the Pope's assertion that the Ptolemaic system was correct in the *Dialogue* and that Copernicanism was wrong. However, Galileo had the Pope's argument for the truth of the (Ptolemaic-)Aristotelian system come from the mouth of the Aristotelian fool, Simplicio, thereby managing to insult the Pope. Urban VIII therefore turned away from his courtier and deemed it necessary that he be punished. The Jesuits welcomed this opportunity to punish Galileo. They had not been able to get him on the charge of Epicurean atomistic heresy in 1624, and *Il dialogo* had no traces of materialist atomism, as *Il saggiatore* had had. But additional reasons for charging Galileo with heresy had to be found, indeed, as it turned out, could be found,

By trial's end, the Roman Inquisition condemned Galileo for being "vehemently suspect of heresy," holding a doctrine contrary to Holy Scriptures, i.e., for being a Copernican. His works were not burned as Nicholas of Autrécourt's were. Instead, they were put in the *Index of Prohibited Books*, and were therefore not to be read by Roman Catholics in any Roman Catholic country, ever.

Neither Galileo nor his friends realized that the attack on the Copernican system in his trial was apparently an artifact for the deeper purpose of attacking the heresy in his *Il saggiatore* eight years after the latter was

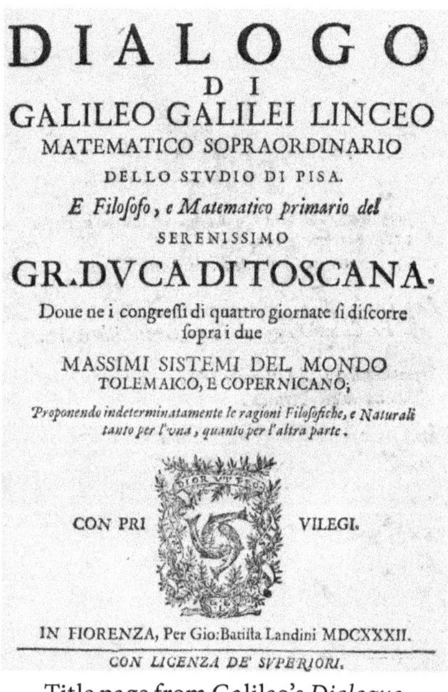

Title page from Galileo's *Dialogue on the Two Great World Systems*

published. (Redondi's book suggests that it was at the heart of the "crime" and heresy of Galileo.) And, an additional factor was the suspicion that Galileo entertained the heretical ideas of Giordano Bruno. Galileo might have suspected that his Copernicanism *per se* was not at the root of his trial and condemnation, had he known, as we saw above, that several Jesuits in the seventeenth century were already trying to explain the Copernican system to scholars at the imperial court in China.[63]

Thus, Galileo might have sensed some deeper subtext was at work in his trial. Indeed, as his trial started, Galileo wrote his friend, Elia Diodati, in Paris:

"I hear from reliable sources that the Jesuit fathers have convinced some very important persons that the *Dialogue on the Two Great World Systems* is execrable and more harmful to the Holy Church than the writings of [Martin] Luther and [John] Calvin."

He continues on January 15, 1633,

"I am sure that [my book] will be prohibited despite the fact that I went to Rome to acquire official permission [*imprimatur*] to publish it and I delivered it personally into the hands of the Master of the Holy Palace [the Pope's theologian, Niccolò Riccardi]."[64]

Might there have been still another reason why Galileo feared his book would run into trouble?

Upon delivery of *The Dialogue on the Two Great World Systems* "into the hands of the Master of the Holy Palace," Niccolò Riccardi, he immediately questioned Galileo about the dolphin emblem on the book's title page. Galileo responded that it was merely the emblem of the book's printer Giovanni Batista Landini, to which Riccardi said, **"If this is true, all will be well."** [My emphasis.]

However, when Galileo could find only some almanacs published by Landini to show Riccardi, they did not contain the dolphin emblem. Consequently Riccardi and, later, the Inquisition could draw only one conclusion: the dolphin emblem must refer to the meaning of Galileo's work itself. Alas, it was only too easy then to construe a meaning that was associated with the heretic Giordano Bruno.[65]

---

63. Sivin 1973.

64. Shea and Artigas 2003, 166.

65. Gosselin and Lerner 1986. However, there were books published by Landini that did use the dolphin emblem, but they could not be found by Galileo to show Riccardi when it would have saved him from the erroneous conclusion that cast Galileo into the unfortunate association with Brunonian heresy.

The association of Galileo's *Dialogue on the Two Great World Systems* with Brunonian meanings was sufficient for the Inquisitors to condemn him. His judges found that Galileo's argument in *The Dialogue* on behalf of the Copernican theory was heretical, and they forced him to recant his Copernican teaching.

Galileo was not condemned to lifelong imprisonment in the Roman Inquisition prison, nor was he burned at the stake. But on June 22, 1633, dressed in the white robes of a penitent, he knelt before the Cardinals Inquisitor, his hand placed on the Bible, and he swore that the Copernican theory was "erroneous and hateful to the Church;" he continued to swear on the Bible that the Ptolemaic-Aristotelian system was, as the Church held, true. His hand still on the Bible, Galileo finally swore that he would never again advocate in word or writing that the heliocentric hypothesis of Copernicus was true.

This is what Cardinal Bellarmine had told Galileo he should do in 1616. Now Galileo finally swore on pain of eternal damnation that he would never again be an apostle of the Copernican theory.

Galileo Galilei was condemned to lifelong imprisonment in his home in the hills across the Arno from the center of Florence, the Villa Il Gioiello in Arcetri. As penance for his vehement heresy, he had to recite the seven Penitential Psalms once weekly for three years (until June 21, 1636). As was normal after any contrite confession, this act of contrition served to cleanse his soul and relieve it from condemnation to Hell, as long as he did not die with any other unconfessed Mortal Sin counted against his soul.

Galileo's daughter, *Suor* Maria Celeste[66], who lived in the Convent of San Matteo, not far from Galileo's villa, took it upon herself to recite these Penitential Psalms for her father. She therefore saved him a quarter of an hour per week on his aging knees.[67] However, Sister Maria Celeste died of dysentery less than ten months after Galileo's condemnation and recantation. Accordingly, for two years and two months and nineteen days more, Galileo himself had to recite these prayers once weekly on his septuagenarian knees.[68]

66. Birth name Virginia Galilei.
67. Sobel 1999, 311-312.
68. Ibid., 345.

Galileo's condemnation occurred on June 22, 1633. Suor Maria Celeste wrote her father every week when he was away from Florence before, during, and after his trial in Rome (including the period after his condemnation and recantation when Urban ViII allowed him to live briefly with Ascanio Piccolimini, the archbishop of Siena). His daughter does not mention in her letters that she was reciting the Penitential Psalms in his stead at this time.[69] It seems that it was only after Galileo's return to Florence in late 1633

Galileo Galilei in 1636
by Justus Sustermans

that she commenced reciting the prayers on his behalf. As she said, it was no great problem, "as she was also praying for sister nuns stricken with disease." Galileo's daughter died on April 2, 1634. Thus she recited the Penitential Psalms for her father for only four months, at most. During the period Galileo resided with the archbishop of Siena and after his daughter's death until the end of his three-year penitential period decreed by the Cardinals Inquisitor on June 21, 1637, Galileo must have recited these psalms once a week, Bible in hand. His knees did indeed feel the pain of penance much more than some historians may have thought.

We now realize that after his daughter's death, Galileo prayed the obligatory psalms for a total of 5,130 minutes until the end of day on June 21, 1637. He kept his promise to the Inquisitors and never again wrote or spoke of Copernicanism. Had he, Galileo could have been declared a lapsed heretic and been condemned to death at the stake. The Catholic Church would have said his soul's punishment would be an eternity in Hell.

Certainly Galileo refrained from advocating the Copernican theory after his 1633 condemnation because of the dire physical punishment that would have awaited him as a lapsed heretic. But one wonders whether Galileo was really sincere in his recantation. He might not have been a sincere Catholic who feared the pains of Hell. He might

---

69. Sobel 2001, 239-339.

only have feared the excruciating pain of death at the stake.

A recent biography argues, in fact, that Galileo was always a good Catholic who "believed in the power of prayer and...tried always to conform his duty as a scientist with the destiny of his soul." And, when the Inquisitors showed him the heresies of which he had been convicted, he found only two items so antithetical to what he believed as a scientist that he could not agree to them. The first said that "he had lapsed in his behavior as a good Catholic," and the other accused him of having acted deceitfully in obtaining the *imprimitur* for the *Dialogue on the Two Great World Systems*. Thus, he would not concede that he was anything but a good Catholic or that he had acted deceitfully.[70] So, finally, because he was a good Catholic, he never wrote on the heliocentric system again.

Galileo did write another dialogue, but it was on mechanics (whose contents are the basis of introductory Physics courses today). It was published under the title of *Discourse and Mathematical Demonstrations on the Two New Sciences*. It was organized in the same way as *The Dialogue on the Two Great World Systems*, and the characters discussing Galileo's mechanics had the same names: Salviati, Salgredo, and Simplicio. In this case, Simplicio was the adherent of Aristotle's kinetics. It was this work that completed Galileo's life-long interest in the study of motion and acceleration which was contrary to Aristotle's writings on the same topics. Since anything he wrote could not be published in Catholic Europe, he found a non-Catholic publisher in a tolerant country: the publishing House of Elzevir in Leiden, The Netherlands.

By the time Galileo died in 1642, he had been under house arrest in Siena and then Florence for nine years. He was completely blind and had been visited by the blind poet John Milton (1608–1674) who, by having written his *Areopagetica*, had become the leading European spokesman for freedom of thought, while Galileo, through his writings and persecution by the Catholic Church, had become the symbol of what happens when religious or state authority condemns free thought and expression.

Because of the 1633 condemnation, when he died Galileo could only be buried in a small side chapel in the Church of Santa Croce

---

70. Sobel 1999, 12 and 275.

in Florence. In 1709, however, through the efforts of
his former secretary and disciple, Vincenzo Viviani, and
Viviani's heirs, Galileo was
reburied with the permission
of Pope Clement XI, in a magnificent tomb along the nave of
Santa Croce. During the movement of his remains, a tooth, a
thumb, a second finger, and a
middle finger were broken off.
These are on permanent display
today in Museo Galileo (until

2010 called the Istituto e Museo di Storia della Scienza).[71] One may
wonder whether there was a special reason why the straight-up middle
finger is featured in the display.

BUT "EPPUR SI MUOVE !"

Galileo is thought to have crossed his fingers as he swore to the
Inquisitors that Earth movement is untrue and said silently, "And yet
it moves." However, this is a fanciful tale. The words were first reported
in 1757 in Giuseppe Marco Antonio Baretti's *The Italian Library*: "The
moment he was set at liberty, he looked up to the sky and down to the
ground, and, stamping with his foot, in a contemplative mood, said
"Eppur si muove."[72]

Facts are facts, never mind the 1633 condemnation. By the time
of Galileo's death, most scientists accepted the fact that the Earth
moves, as do the other planets, around the Sun. The ultimate issue
that brought about the final acceptance of the Copernican theory
was stellar parallax. If the Earth orbited the Sun, as Copernicus and
Galileo argued, then the moving Earth required that the stars be
seen at different angles, and the universe should be much larger than
the Ancients had believed. After the time of Sir Isaac Newton (1643–
1727) telescopes became more sophisticated and in 1838 Friedrich

71. Livio 2020a, Ch. 15, n. 211.
72. Livio 2020b.

Bessel (1784–1846) made the first successful parallax measurement. After that point, no careful thinker, not even in the Roman Catholic Church, could deny the achievements of Galileo and the truth of Copernican heliocentrism for our solar system, and indeed for all other solar systems in the universe.

"And yet...." The state, the church, or whatever other group can force denial of truth. But facts are facts, truth is truth. Whether or not Galileo mumbled the above words as he was forced to adjure the truth of the Copernican and Galilean Sun-centered model of our solar system, the "and yet" is true. Truth stands above all things.

Religious forces in the Middle Ages and Renaissance fought against the truth of astronomical science, just as in more recent times various religious and political groups have fought and fight against Darwinism, the Flat Earthers against the realization that the Earth is a sphere (even though scientists have held the earth's sphericity ever since the time of Hipparchus), while others have argued against medicine and epidemiology today.[73] These groups form the category of Science Deniers that Mario Livio and several other scientists have written about.[74]

Pope John Paul II had the Secret Archives of the Vatican opened up to reexamine the Galileo Trial. That was the first great science denier case. The conclusion of this modern investigation was that "the whole question of the relationship between science and faith... may be serenely and objectively considered and brought to the rightful conclusion."[75]

"Serene and objective reconsideration"

"Serene and objective reconsideration" took a long time. Galileo was condemned on June 22, 1633. Finally, on November 4, 1992, Pope John Paul II decreed that the 1633 condemnation of Galileo had been a "historical error."[76]

After three hundred fifty-nine years, the Roman Catholic Church, at its highest level, had finally accepted the truth of the lesson that

---

73. Weill 2023.

74. Livio, 2020a.

75. Pagano, 1984, x.

76. [Pope John Paul II]. *L'Osservatore Romano*. November 4, 1992.

Galileo Galilei had tried to teach its theologians in *The Letter to the Grand Duchess* in 1615.

I hope that the truths of science will one day be accepted by all.

SUMMARIZING PART A

The main problem with Copernicus's and Galileo's world view was their commitment to the uniform circular motion of the Earth and the other planets around the Sun, a commitment which had prevented Copernicus from reducing the number of epicycles he used from those used by Ptolemy. This problem was solved by Johannes Kepler who proved that the planets' motions form ellipses around the Sun.

This, in fact, is almost what Ptolemy of Alexandria (fl. 150 CE) had achieved by introducing the equant point. Or, to put it more accurately, Ptolemy's equant point model's success was due to something he could not have known. As Asger Aaboe writes,

> "[Ptolemy's equant point] shared a certain property of Keplerian motion — That if you observe a planet not from the Sun, but from the other, empty focus of its orbit,...then the planet will seem to travel very nearly uniformly around you.... The kind of motion Ptolemy employed on the deferent of his equant model is a very good approximation to a Keplerian motion of a planet around the Sun with the Sun at the observer's place O, the eccentricity of the circle the same as the ellipse's, and the empty focus as the equant point Q.... So we have seen that Ptolemy was on the right track when he abandoned uniform circular motion, philosophically incorrect though it was [according to Aristotle's teachings] and long remained, and replaced it with a circular motion about a point other than the center [Earth]."[77]

We should note that Kepler's law of uniform motion came after his deep study of ancient mathematical and astronomical texts on the geometry of the ellipse, *viz.*, Archimedes (c. 287–212 BCE) and Apollonius (fl. 200 BCE). Both Ptolemy and, centuries later, Kepler studied these texts. Ptolemy's and Kepler's ideas on ellipses and conic

---

77. Aaboe 2001, 136 and 164-5, and Figure 15 (p. 166).

sections derived from these ancient mathematicians and therefore they were similar to each other, as we have said.[78]

We can understand why, before Kepler, many Renaissance astronomers did not rush to accept Copernicanism. Without Kepler's innovation, Copernicanism did not actually offer an acceptable alternative to the Scholastic phiosophers' adherence to the Aristotelian system. Kepler's innovation allowed him to achieve the escape from pure circular planetary motion that Ptolemy had achieved.

We have discussed, in the section on the Panofsky thesis,[79] why Galileo also could not accept what Kepler had achieved. We pointed out, further, that Galileo's *Dialogue on the Two Great World Systems* did not really address any aspect of the Ptolemaic system. Copernicanism was, without Kepler, a weak reed, a point most historians of science seem not to realize. The very fact that Copernicus and Galileo were heroes, creators, of the Scientific Revolution means that it is all too easy to forget the achievements of the earlier Babylonian and Hellenistic astronomers (if they were understood at all) as they applauded Copernicus's and Galileo's achievements.

Exact mathematical astronomy existed, as we have seen, in ancient Babylon and Uruk, as well as in the astronomy of Ptolemy of Alexandria. The Scientific Revolution commenced with these first Starry Messengers.

B. THE CHEMICAL REVOLUTION JOINS THE MECHANICAL AND ASTRONOMICAL REVOLUTIONS

One of the problems of Thomas Kuhn's *Structure of Scientific Revolution* is that, when he discussed the "first scientific revolution," he did not argue that there had been a previous paradigm, although that should have been the logic of his argument. How then can something, science in this case, be overturned and replaced by a new scientific paradigm? In fact, the term "Scientific Revolution" might best not be used. I think we should construe science as an ever-innovating and developing process since it first began along the Tigris and Euphrates Rivers.

---

78. For a complete technical discussion, read Aaboe 2001, 135-70 ["Kepler Motion Viewed from Either Focus"].

79. pp. 109–110 above.

As we have seen in Section A, exact mathematical astronomical science did exist since about 350 BCE and then, in the second century CE, the Ptolemaic System with its equant point, so much criticized by modern historians of science, was actually very much like Kepler's seventeenth-century elliptical orbits with their empty *foci*.

Now we turn to what another historian of science, Allen G. Debus, late of the University of Chicago, called the Chemical Revolution. It started with the alchemist Paracelsus and culminated with Sir Isaac Newton. But it, too, is not unlike the process that began with horoscopic omens and developed into the mathematical exactitude of planetary ephemerides like the ephemeris for mul-babbar that we discussed earlier.

The so-called Scientific Revolution of the sixteenth and seventeenth centuries has been equated with the astronomical, mechanical, and philosophical changes wrought by Copernicus, Galileo, Kepler, and, later, Newton. However, there was a contemporaneous "scientific revolution" that competed with the mechanistic one that was first made famous by Eduard Jan Dijksterhuis's *Mecharisering van het wereldbeeld* (*The Mechanization of the World Picture*[80]).

The Chemical Revolution was separate from the mechanistic one of Galileo[81] and the more astronomical ones of Copernicus and Kepler. We often think of Newton as heir to Copernicus, Galileo, and Kepler, but we shall see that Newton was equally heir to this so-called Chemical Revolution. This last revolution was sired by the "chemical philosophy" of the German philosopher Phillipus Aureolus Theophrastus von Hohenheim, better known as Paracelsus (1493–1541)[82].

Paracelsus by Quentin Matsys

---

80. First published in Dutch in 1950 and published in English in 1961.

81. The "revolution" in mechanics was achieved in Galileo's *Discourses and Mathematical Demonstrations Relating to Two New Sciences*.

82. Debus 1996.

While Paracelsus's alchemical thought was directly related to iatrochemistry (alchemy and medicine), it also had a profound influence on Isaac Newton (1643–1727). Although Newton never published them, modern scholars such as Frank E. Manuel and Betty Jo Teeter Dobbs have explored his many religious and alchemical writings.[83] These studies, especially those by Dobbs, have shown that most of Isaac Newton's time was spent stoking his alchemical ovens and writing the results of his experi-

Isaac Newton at 46
by Godfrey Kneller, 1689

ments therein. Dobbs has estimated that probably only 15% of Newton's working time was devoted to what we would today call physics and astronomy, while roughly 85% was devoted to alchemical experiments as well as to his Old Testament chronological studies. This fact does nothing to deny Newton's scientific genius, but it is important for the student of the history of science to realize what Newton himself was trying to achieve. It was not what physics textbooks would lead the physics student to think. As Dobbs said,

> "With the post-Newtonian diminution of interest in divinity and heightened interest in nature for its own sake, scholars have too often read the Newtonian method narrowly, selecting from the breadth of his studies only mathematics, experiment, observation, and reason as the essential components of his scientific method.... One result of the restricted interests of modernity has been to look askance at Newton's biblical, [Old Testament] chronological, and alchemical studies: to consider his pursuit of *prisca sapientia* [ancient wisdom] as irrelevant.... [Newton's] goal was Truth, and for this he utilized every possible resource."[84]

---

83. Newton's alchemical manuscripts are housed mainly in Trinity College, Cambridge University, and the Yahuda Collection in the Jewish National and University Library, Jerusalem.

84. Dobbs 1991, 7.

Newton's goal, successful in his mind, was to show that the alchemical writers of Antiquity were the progenitors of his most famous scientific discovery, the Law of Gravity. He believed that the mechanical laws of science (Galileo's, Kepler's, and his own) led to the same scientific conclusions and understandings as the conclusions of the wise men of ancient times.

Dobbs also called Isaac Newton a "Janus figure," meaning that he looked both forward and backward in time. He was forward looking in that he completed the work of the "Copernican Revolution." He looked forward to what might be called the Newtonian paradigm that governed science from the early eighteenth to the early twentieth centuries. He was backward looking because he believed in the Neoplatonic doctrine of the unity of all Truth, including the truth of alchemy and the *Hermetica*.[85]

Isaac Newton believed that the universe was governed by an animistic spirit, a living soul which explained the universe's ongoing existence and laws. Indeed, by the mid 1670s, Newton argued that the universe was ruled by a "living, most subtle Aether." He said that he had discovered its description in ancient, alchemical texts (such as *The Emerald Tablet* which he had translated from Latin to English, as well as described in his own alchemical experiments). It was this Aether that prevented his universe from being materialistic like the French philosopher René Descartes' "closed mechanical universe."[86]

Although Newton continued the achievements of Galileo's mechanics in his own *Mathematical Principles of Natural Philosophy*, otherwise known as the *Principia* (1687), and in his *Opticks* (1704), he wanted to show how the Law of Gravity was governed by the Paracelsian art of alchemy. He believed that Gravity was God's Viceroy and that Gravity governed the entire universe, and that the ancient alchemical texts had actually predicted the Law of Gravity long before he discovered it in a mathematical and physical formulation. Newton was always hunting for the alchemical law of the "Greene Lyon" which would reveal, he said, what the Ancients called "the pipes of Pan," an alchemical law that would bind the Universe together. In other words, this was the way God governed the Universe through the viceroyship of the "subtle

---

85. Ibid., passim.
86. Dobbs 1991, 5 and elsewhere.

Aether." And this "Greene Lyon," Viceroy of the universe, was Gravity When Newton said that his own "scientific achievements" were based on the "shoulders of giants," he not only meant the likes of Galileo, Kepler, and Copernicus. He equally meant the Neoplatonic, Hermetic, and alchemical philosophers of Antiquity and the Renaissance. Moreover, when we unpack his formula for the Law of Gravity, we also find that our Sun binds together by its power not just our own solar system but the entire, infinite universe. Our Sun plays the role of God's Governor. It is the ultimate derivation of the Solar Age of the Renaissance.[87]

NEWTON'S RELIGION AND THE LAW OF GRAVITY

Newton never had trouble with the Church of England in the way that Galileo had with the Church of Rome. This was not because Anglicanism was more tolerant than Roman Catholicism. Newton's theological beliefs seriously diverted from Anglican orthodoxy. His theological core belief was similar to late-ancient Arianism because he denied the doctrine of Christ's divinity that had been established at the ecumenical Council of Nicaea in 325 CE. The main reason why Newton's unorthodoxy never caused the English theological authorities to prosecute him for this (or any other) heresy was that he kept his heretical beliefs to himself and in texts that he wrote but never published.

By 1750 and after, scientists were unaware of Newton's work in alchemy and his biblical commentaries. They read only his published works (his *Principia* and *Opticks*), and his laws of motion and gravitation. His almost total absorption with alchemy and biblical studies were not part of the Newtonianism that modern scientists have known or studied.

However, the premodern part of the Janus-like Newton, the alchemical Newton, did remain in modern science texts in two ways that were not realized until contemporary historians of science and intellectual historians discovered Newton's total body of manuscripts. First, until the late nineteenth century, scientists still thought that the Earth was surrounded by Newton's "most subtle or luminous Aether" and, second, that the law of gravity was applicable to any and every part of the universe because the "Lord God" governed the universe by "Active

---

87. Cf. Garin, 1958.

Principles," *viz.*, by the "viceroyship" of our Sun. This latter idea, though not understood by modern scientists, was embedded in Newton's formula of the law of gravitation. Both these ideas were holdovers from the Solar Age, at the end of which period Newton thought and wrote. In the General Scholium to the second edition of the *Principia* (1713),

> "Newton 'universalized' his solar law of attraction and applied it to the attraction of any two bodies or particles in the universe...at any distance from each other in the infinite universe....[It is based on Newton's use of] the universal constant G which is...based on Kepler's Third harmonic law [and uses] M, the mass of our solar system's Sun."[88]

The Harvard historian of science, I. Bernard Cohen, said that "There is no mathematics...to justify Newton's bold step" of applying the mass of our Sun as the vital point in the universal law of attraction.[89] No mathematics, indeed, but rather there was the philosophical tradition of the power of the Sun, described as an active agent of God, which lasted from the Renaissance Neoplatonist philosophers at least to Newton's 1713 *Principia*.

THE END OF NEWTON'S "SUBTLE AETHER"

The belief in Newton's principle of the Aether came to an end in 1887 with the Michelson-Morley Experiments in Cleveland, Ohio.

In April to July 1887, Albert A. Michelson and Edward W. Morley performed a series of experiments at what is now Case Western Reserve University. Michelson and Morley compared the speed of light in perpendicular directions to see if there was a difference in the relative motion of matter as it passed in these different directions, as there should have been if it was passing through the "subtle and luminous Aether" that Newton spoke of. There was **no** difference; it was a negative outcome. Their published result was positive proof that there was no "Aether wind." This last Newtonian "spook" had been overthrown, making possible the next step in replacing the Newtonian scientific paradigm with another paradigm in the twentieth century. This new paradigm was made possible by Albert Einstein (1879–1955). His *Special*

88. Gosselin 1991, 56-7.
89. Cohen 1985, 167.

Theory of Relativity (1905) retained Newton's laws for objects moving at "slow velocities," but Newtonian laws were not able to be used with objects approaching the speed of light (186,000 mi/sec).

Einstein had been aware of Michelson and Morley's work before he wrote his paper on "The Electrodynamics of Electricity," in which he stated his Theory of Special Relativity, for he had already read *Attempt at a Theory of Electrical and Optical Phenomena in Moving Bodies*

Albert Einstein in 1905

by the Danish physicist Hendrik Lorentz (1853–1928). In this book, Lorentz discussed a series of failed attempts to find the Aether, including the last and most convincing one by the two physicists in Cleveland. In later lectures, as he aged, Einstein variously claimed both to have been influenced by the Michelson-Morley experiments and also not to have known about them. The latter assertion may well have been the result of advancing age. The truth of the matter is that the Michelson-Morley Experiments removed the Aether as a phenomenon through which light and bodies had to move, and made Special Relativity and all of post-Newtonian science in the twentieth and twenty-first centuries possible.[90]

SUMMING UP

All those who studied the planets and stars from the time of the Mesopotamians until Galileo could see them only with human eyes. For the first time, Galileo observed the Earth's moon and discovered the moons of Jupiter with his crude but adequate telescope. Ever since then, telescopes have become ever more powerful instruments, until the present day when the James Webb Space Telescope, orbiting the Sun, about a million miles away from Earth, sends us the most extraordinary images of stars and galaxies from 13.6 billion years ago (about 100 to 250 million years after the Big Bang). This brings us very close to actually seeing the vital moment, the beginning of the universe. The Starry

90. Isaacson 2008, 116-7.

Messengers are no longer Scribes hoping for cloudless nights to peer into the skies, but technological wonders like the Hubble Telescope and the even more powerful JWST made by Northrop Grumman and Ball Aerospace and Technologies. Trained scientists can now download these images coming from a deep space they themselves can't see.

Let's Finally Consider Our Long-Time and Present Abode, the Earth

First off, ancient Mesopotamian mythology held that the Earth was flat, with the sky in the shape of a dome above it. This belief was displaced by Greek and Hellenistic astronomers who'd believed that Earth, the place from which we observe the universe, is a sphere.

The belief in the sphericity of the Earth has been held by all people ever since, through the darkest days of the early Middle Ages, through the Twelfth-Century Renaissance and the Scholastic theologians and philosophers, through the Renaissance and the so-called Scientific Revolution, to our own time.[91]

In the nineteenth century, scientists determined that there is a flattening to the Earth's roundness, making it an ellipsoid, not a perfect sphere. The flattening of the Earth's surface was thought to be about 1/300. Today, the United States Department of Defense Geodetic System calculates the figure at 1/298.25. So our Earth is ever so slightly more in the shape of a pear than of a soccer ball.[92]

Still, we can say that the Earth is basically round. And Western people have been in agreement that the Earth is round and not flat since about the third century BCE. Yet textbooks and some teachers have said that Columbus set out to prove the Earth is round. He did not have to prove this to the King and Queen of Spain by holding an egg up to them. They knew it already. Nor was Newton suddenly persuaded of the Earth's sphericity and gravity when an apple fell on his head, as other fanciful tales have said.[93]

91. However, in the twentieth and twentieth-first centuries, there did develop a group of people who believe in the Flat Earth. One constructed a backyard rocket so he could ascend and prove there is no curvature to the Earth. Needless to say, his rough-hewn rocket and his ascent in it failed. Founded in 1956, the Flat Earth Society has had as many as 3,500 members. See Pappas 2021 and Weill 2023.

92. Gosselin 1985, Notes.

93. Numbers 2015, who discusses these and other scientific myths.

So it is a major wonder to me that there are people in the United States and elsewhere today who belong to the Flat Earth Society; that there are politicians, religious leaders, everyday folks who now believe the Earth is flat.

These are the same types who also deny clear scientific evidence about Climate Change, and refuse to do anything to halt the dangerous increase in Earth's temperature that is caused by the continued use of fossil fuels; nor to prevent what will continue to happen as the ice on the Earth's poles melts, as the oceans rise and make life more and more unlivable along continental and island coasts, and in great and lesser oceanside cities like Miami, Los Angeles, and New York, and Seal Beach and Monterey, California. These are some of the results we can clearly predict as a result of Climate Change. Will humans have to leave our Earth? If we do, it will become just another lonely planetary body in the universe and our descendants will have moved to another far-off home. We will explore this scenario in our next chapter.

Chapter Four Select Bibliography

GENERAL

Ball 2012: Philip Ball. *Curiosity: How Science Became Interested in Everything.* Chicago: University of Chicago Press, 2012.

Gombrich 1986: E. H. Gombrich. *Aby Warburg: An Intellectual Biography.* Chicago: University of Chicago Press, 1986.

Dijksterhuis 1961: Eduard Jan Dijksterhuis. *The Mechanization of the World Picture.* Princeton, NJ: Princeton University Press, 1961/1986.

Hazard 2013: Paul Hazard *The European Mind: 1680–1715.* New York: New York Review of Books Classic, 2013.

Kuhn 1962: Thomas S. Kuhn. *The Structure of Scientific Revolutions.* Chicago: University of Chicago Press, 1962.

Numbers 2015: Ronald Numbers. *Newton's Apple and Other Myths about Science.* Cambridge, MA: Harvard University Press, 2015.

Santillana 1955: Giorgio de Santillana. *The Crime of Galileo.* Chicago: University of Chicago Press, 1955.

Shapin 1998: Steven Shapin. *The Scientific Revolution.* Chicago: University of Chicago Press, 1998.

750 BCE to 1453 CE

Aaboe 1963: Asger Aaboe. *Episodes from the Early History of Mathematics.* New York: New Mathematical Library, Vol. 13, 1963.

Aaboe 2001: Asger Aaboe. *Episodes from the Early History of Astronomy.* New York: Springer, 2001.

Autrecourt 1971: Nicholas of Autrecourt. *The Universal Treatise.* Leonard A. Kennedy, Richard E. Arnold, Arthur E. Millard, translators. Milwaukee, WI: Marquette University Press, 1971.

Chiera 1966: Edward Chiera. *They Wrote on Clay.* Chicago: University of Chicago Press, 1938/1966.

Dante 1970: Dante Alighieri. *The Divine Comedy* (1308-1320). Translated by John Ciardi. New York: New American Library, 1970.

Euclid 1956: Euclid of Alexandria. *The Thirteen Books of Euclid's Elements.* Translated from the text of Johan Ludwig Heiberg, with introduction and commentary by Sir Thomas L. Heath. 3 Vols. New York: Dover, Publications, 1956.

Goldstein 1967: Bernard R. Goldstein. "The Arabic Version of Ptolemy's *Planetary Hypotheses." Transcripts of the American Philosophical Society.* N.S. 57, 4 (1967).

Gosselin 1985 Notes. Edward A. Gosselin. Notes from NEH Yale Seminar on the Exact Sciences in Antiquity and the Middle Ages, Asger Aoboe, Director. Yale,1985.

Koyré 1957. Alexandre Koyré. *From the Closed World to the Infinite Universe.* Baltimore, MD, The John's Hopkins University Press, 1957.

Neugebauer 1955: Otto Neugebauer. ACT: *Astronomical Cuneiform Texts.* New York: Springer, 1955.

Neugebauer 1969: Otto Neugebauer. *The Exact Sciences in Antiquity.* Providence, RI: Brown University Press, 1957; reprint Dover, 1969.

Neugebauer 1975: Otto Neugebauer. *A History of Ancient Mathematical Astronomy.* 3 Vols. New York: Springer, 1975.

Neugebauer 1983: Otto Neugebauer. *History and Astronomy.* New York: Springer, 1983.

Oosterhoff 2015: Richard J. Oosterhoff. "A Book, a Pen, and the *Sphere*: Reading Sacrobosco in the Renaissance." *History of Universities,* Vol. XXVIII/2. Oxford, UK: Oxford University Press, 2015.

Pedersen 2009. Olaf Pedersen. *Early Physics and Astronomy.* Cambridge, UK/New York: Cambridge University Press Digital Version, 2009.

Sachs and Neugebauer 1945: A. J. Sachs and Otto Neugebauer. *Mathematical Cuneiform Texts.* New Haven, CT: Yale University Press, 1945.

Sachs 1955. A. J. Sachs. "A Classification of the Babylonian Astronomical Tablets of the Seleucid Period." *Journal of Cuneiform Studies*, II, 271-90.

Swerdlow 1983: Noel M. Swerdlow. *The Babylonian Theory of the Planets*. Princeton, NJ: Princeton University Press, 1983.

Toomer 1984: G. J. Toomer. *Ptolemy's* Almagest. New York: Springer, 1984.

Van der Waerden 1974: B. L. Van der Waerden. *Science Awakening: The Birth of Astronomy*. Vol. 2. Leyden: Noordhoff International Publishing/Oxford, UK: Oxford University Press, 1974.

1453 CE to 1905 CE

Biagioli 1993: Mario Biagioli. *Galileo Courtier: The Practice of Science in the Culture of Absolutism*. Chicago: University of Chicago Press, 1993.

Bruno 1584a: *The Ash Wednesday Supper* (*La cena de le Ceneri*, 1584). Translated and edited by Edward A. Gosselin and Lawrence S. Lerner. Toronto: University of Toronto Press, 1985.

Bruno 1584b: *Lo spaccio della bestia trionfante*. Paris [*sic*: read London], 1584.

Christianson 1984: Gale E. Christianson.*In the Presence of the Creator: Isaac Newton and His Times*. New York: The Free Press, 1984.

Cohen 1985: I. Bernard Cohen. *The Birth of a New Physics*. New York: W. W. Norton and Company, 1985.

Debus 1996: Allen G. Debus. *Paracelso e la traditions Paracelsiano*. Naples, Italy: Istituto Italians per gli Studi Filosofici (Città del Solee), 1996.

Dobbs 1975: Betty Jo Teeter Dobbs. *The Foundation of Newton's Alchemy or "The Hunting of the Greene Lyon."* Cambridge, UK: Cambridge University Press, 1975.

Dobbs 1991: *The Janus Faces of Genius: The Role of Alchemy in Newton's Thought*. Cambridge, UK: Cambridge University Press.1991.

Drake 2001: Stillman Drake. *Galileo: A Very Short Biography*. Oxford, UK: Oxford University Press, 2001.

Ferguson 2002: *Tycho and Kepler: The Unlikely Partnership that Forever Changed Our Understanding of the Heavens*. New York: Walker and Company, 2002.

Ficino 1493: Marsilio Ficino. *De sole et lumine*. Firenze, Italia: Antonio di Bartolommeo Miscomini, 1493.

Garin 1958: Eugenio Garin. *Studi sul platonismo médiévale*. Firenze, Italia: Felice Monnier, 1958.

Giglioni 2017: Guido Giglioni. "Germana Ernst (1943–2016)." *Isis*, 108/4 (December 2017), 852-4.

Gingrich 2004: Owen Gingrich. *The Book Nobody Read: Chasing the Revolutions of Nicolaus Copernicus*. New York: Walker and Company, 2004.

Gosselin 1991: Edward A. Gosselin. "The Lord God's Sun in Pico della Mirandola's and Sir Isaac Newton." *Renaissance Society and Culture: Essays in Honor of Eugene F. Rice, Jr.* John Monfasani and Ronald G. Mufstafa, Editors. New York: Italica Press, 1991.

Gosselin and Lerner 1975: Edward A. Gosselin and Lawrence S. Lerner. "Galileo and the Long Shadow of Bruno." *Archives Internationales d'Histoire des Sciences*, XXXV/9 (1975).

Gosselin and Lerner 1986: Edward A. Gosselin and Lawrence S. Lerner. "Galileo and the Specter of Bruno." *Scientific American*, 254/11 (November, 1986), 126-33.

Isaacson 2008: Walter Isaacson. *Einstein: His Life and the Universe*. New York: Simon and Schuster, 2008.

Koyré 1958: Alexandre Koyré. *From the Closed World to the Infinite Universe*. Baltimore, MD: The Johns Hopkins University Press, 1958.

Koyré 1965: Alexandre Koyré. *Newtonian Studies*. Cambridge, MA: Harvard University Press, 1965.

Lerner and Gosselin 1973: Lawrence S. Lerner and Edward A. Gosselin. "Giordano Bruno." *Scientific American* (April 1973).

Livio 2020a: Mario Livio. *Galileo and the Science Deniers.* New York: Simon & Schuster Paperbacks, 2020.

Livio 2020b: Mario Livio. "Did Galileo Truly Say, 'And Yet It Moves'?" *Scientific American* (May 6, 2020s).

[Pope John Paul II]. *L'Osservatore Romano 1992.* Vatican City, November 4, 1992.

Martinez 2016: Albert A. Martinez, "Giordano Bruno and the Heresy of Many Worlds," *Annals of Science*, 2073/4 (2016), 45-74.

Pagano 1984: Sergio Pagano, Editor. *I documents del processo di Galileo Galilei.* Collectanea Archivi Vaticana 21: Città del Vaticano: Archivio Vaticano, 1984.

Panofsky 1956: "Galileo as a Critic of the Arts: Aesthetic Attitude and Scientific Thought." *Isis*, 47/1 (March, 1956), 3-15.

Pappas 2021: Stephanie Pappas, "Are the Flat-earthers Serious," *Live Science* (Dec.16, 2021)

Pico 1969: Giovanni Pico della Mirandola. *Heptaplus*, in *Opera omnia* I:55. Hildesheim, Germany: Georg Olms, 1969.

Redondi 1987: Pietro Redondi, *Galileo Heretic.* Translated by Raymond Rosenthal. Princeton, NJ: Princeton University Press, 1987.

Shea and Artigas 2003: William R. Shea and Mariano Artigas. *Galileo in Rome: The Rise and Fall of a Troublesome Genius.* Oxford, UK: Oxford University Press, 2003.

Sivin 1973: Nathan Sivin (also known as Xiwen). "Copernicus in China." *Studia Copernica.* Warsaw, Poland: 1973.

Sobel 1999: Dava Sobel. *Galileo's Daughter: A Historical Memoir of Science, Faith, and Love.* New York: Walker and Company, 1999.

Sobel 2001: Dava Sobel, *Letters to Father: Suor Maria Celeste to Galileo, 1623-1633.* New York: Walker and Company, 2001.

Swerdlow and Neugebauer 1974/2012: N. M. Swerdlow and O. Neugebauer. *Mathematical Astronomy in Copernicus's De revolutionibus.* 2 vols. New York: Springer, 1974/2012.

Webster 2008: Charles Webster. *Paracelsus: Medicine, Magic, and Mission at the End of Time.* New Haven, CT: Yale University Press, 2008.

Waddington 1973: Raymond B. Waddington. "The Sun at the Center: Structure and Meaning in Pico della Mirandola's *Heptaplus.*" *Journal of Medieval and Renaissance Studies,* 3 (1973), 69-86.

Weill 2023: Kathy Weill. *Off the Edge: Flat Earthers, Conspiracy Culture, and Why People Will Believe Anything.* Chapel Hill, NC: Algonquin Press, 2023.

Westman 2011: Robert S. Westman. *The Copernican Question: Prognostication, Skepticism, and Celestial Order.* Berkeley and Los Angeles, CA: University of California Press, 2011.

Yates 1947: Frances A. Yates. *The French Academies of the Sixteenth Century.* London: Warburg Institute, 1947/Routledge, 1989.

Yates 1964: Frances A. Yates. *Giordano Bruno and the Hermetic Tradition.* Chicago: University of Chicago Press, 1964.

And Beyond to 2117 CE

Rutherford 2017: Bill Rutherford. "Brave New Worlds." New York: *Columbia Magazine.* Winter-Spring, 2017.

Eiseley 1959: Loren Eiseley. *The Immense Journey: An Imaginative Naturalist Explores the Mysteries of Man and Nature.* New York: Vintage, 1959.

Gosselin 2018: Edward A. Gosselin. "A History for Our Times." An Unpublished Essay on the Move of the Human Race to *Proxima Centauri b,* the Next Earth. Jacksonville, OR, 2018.

Pappas 2021: Stephanie Pappas. "Are Flat-Earthers Being Serious." *Live Science.* December 16, 2021.

EPILOGUE

A HISTORY
OF THE FUTURE

Prologue

On Our Way to
Proxima Centauri b

Jules Verne's *From the Earth to the Moon* (1874), the *Star Trek* movies, and NASA's astronauts who landed on the moon have made us think that man can travel to planets within our solar system and even in the universe. These books, movies, and scientific-technological achievements have led to the point where we even think that those who are wealthy enough to pay for a trip in a space ship going around the Earth in nearby space can also travel in space.

The Climate Change crisis which now threatens the Earth and humans' lives on it has created a situation where millions or billions of humans may have to be transported outside our solar system to another planet, an exoplanet, that will become the permanent abode of our descendants. This will not be an easy journey or an easy transformation in our living conditions. And these descendants will all be immigrants to this new planet, no matter what country they came from on Earth.

This chapter is *A History of the Future*, a prediction to be sure, but perhaps one that will come to pass when humans have landed and begun settlement on Proxima Centauri b.

A History of the Future

We are in the midst of a Climate Change crisis. Global temperature since 1880 has risen 1.0° degrees Celsius (1.8° Fahrenheit). This temperature rise has been largely caused by man's industries, especially those used for heating and for operating automobiles and trucks. There are ways to halt the ongoing temperature rise, such as shutting down coal mines and ending the fossil fuel operation of vehicles. In exchange, we can use wind energy, solar energy, hydroelectric power, and even nuclear power. But the success of these alternatives to fossil fuels depends on the willingness of people and governments to make these changeovers. Not all governments have made the necessary efforts to effect such changes: China, India, and the Republican-governed United States are examples.

The likelihood, then, is that global temperatures will continue to rise. A global increase of 2°-3° Celsius is not unlikely. As this happens, polar ice caps will completely melt, the oceans will swell, coastal cities may have to be in part or even completely abandoned, and more and more monster storms will occur. In the USA, the central food belt of the country may no longer be able to produce the nation's food, let alone vegetables and wheat for other parts of the world. We can foresee mass movements of people to areas which can still produce food and struggles between those who live in these areas and those who are seeking settlement in the regions that still can produce needed foods. There is also a real possibility of the extinction of the human race unless resettlement can occur on another planet.[1]

Given the likelihood that the Climate Crisis will not abet, it's no wonder that in 2017 the distinguished physicist Stephen Hawking urged humans to leave Earth "in a hundred years or so."[2] The target year for leaving Earth is therefore 2117. One can imagine that several major

---

1. See Lenton, et al. The authors argue that by the end of the twenty-first century Earth's temperature will be between 2-2.7° C higher than before industrialization, and that this will come at a moral cost that should be examined. The most extreme global warming will occur around the Equator, causing poorer people to move toward the poles. Richer people living in still habitable parts of the planet will try to keep them out of those regions.

2. Stephen Hawking, quoted in CNBC on line, May 5, 2017. Also You Tube -Yahoo, May 4, 2017.

nations will try to create "space buses" of sufficient size to carry large cargoes of humans to another planet, an exoplanet outside our solar system, Those planning these mass exits would try to move millions, if not billions, of people to the closest exoplanet. The closest one that is similarly close to its star as is the Earth to our Sun is Proxima Centauri b, in the constellation Centaurus.[3]

The magnitude of the problem in transporting the human race to Proxima b can be seen by its distance from Earth. It is 2.42 light years from Earth, meaning that it will take 6300 years, using current technology. Algorithms have already been determined[4] as to the size of the settlers or breeding pairs needed for each outer space voyage and their capacity to reproduce successfully without excessive inbreeding: 49 breeding pairs are needed when each space bus launches for the chance of a successful arrival. Many generations will be born, live and die on each space bus between launch and set down. There will, of course be some technical problems incurred by the space busses that will cause failures and a certain amount of disease among the settlers on board that will lead to premature death. And only the first generation at take off and the last generation at touchdown will have any knowledge of Earth, in the first place, and of Proxima b, in the last case. All the other generations will be cognizant only of their space busses.

Clearly, the voyages from Earth to Proxima b will be a monumental task in and of themselves. Those passengers who arrive will face new complexities. The planet's landscape will be undeveloped, if not barren. No signs of civilized life will exist. All foodstuffs will have to be grown from scratch, and the best one can hope for are caves in which to live. In other words, social, political, and economic life for humans will have to begin anew, as if from Stone Age times.

Stephen Hawking said humans, facing extinction, will have to leave Earth some time around 2117.[5] If this is true, it is because of humans' failure at their stewardship of our Earth. In hundreds of thousands of years, will our race fail once again on our new planet, Prima Centauri b?[6]

---

3. Centaurus can be seen in the Southern Hemisphere.

4. MIT Technology Review (June 22, 2018).

5. Hawking later said we'd have to leave Earth in 200 years and, at another time 600 years. Whichever time it might be, the problems outlined here will be the same.

6. Since publication, see Scoles 2023 on difficulties of humans living in space.

Epilogue Select Bibliography

Lenton et al. 2023: Thomas M. Lenton, et al, "Quantifying the Human Cost of Global Warming." *Nature Sustainability.* May 23, 2023.

MIT 2018: *MIT Technology Review.* June 22, 2018.

Scoles 2023: Sarah Scoles. "Why We'll Never Live in Space." *Scientific American.* October 2023.

Post Scriptum

The Clarity of
Thought and Truth

We have delved into five different topics in this book. Although they do not solve any of our present problems, they do show us that the human experience, as we delve into nation building, sexuality, philosophical belief, science, and even exoplanet exploration, can lead to the solution of problems we humans face. We can succeed if we follow Galileo's dictum: "All truths are easy to understand once they are discovered; the point is to discover them." My training, my mentors, my colleagues, and my teaching have convinced me that historical interpretation can, like Galileo's science, be based on truth. Or, to put it in a somewhat different way, the lesson we all can learn from the story of my cat Blackie is that we should seek human truth above all things and forego false fables. If we always seek truth in science as well as in all human affairs, there will be hope for mankind.

Edward Alberic Gosselin
Jacksonville, Oregon, January, 2024

ABOUT THE AUTHOR

Edward Alberic Gosselin is Emeritus Professor of History at California State University, Long Beach, where he taught for thirty-four years. He served as History Department Chair and as Editor of the Society for History Education's journal, *The History Teacher*. He has also been a visiting Emeritus Professor at Southern Oregon University.

Dr. Gosselin is a graduate of Yale University (BA) and Columbia University (MA and PhD). His specialities are Renaissance and Reformation history, the history of science, modernization theory, twentieth-century French historiography, and the decolonization of the British Empire. He is a former Fulbright Research Scholar in France.

Dr. Gosselin has been an academic-year Fellow at the National Humanities Institute at the University of Chicago, and has held summer fellowships at Stanford University, Yale University, and at the University of Texas, Austin.

He lives in Jacksonville, Oregon, with his wife, Jois Harkness, and their two dogs.

www.ingramcontent.com/pod-product-compliance
Lightning Source LLC
Chambersburg PA
CBHW061130160726
48006CB00036B/1577